Foreword...

My name is Frank Swanson, and I am a teacher. Like most in the profession, I fucking hate it. Since the odds of winning the lottery challenge my limited math skills, I figure writing a book might be my ticket out. I belong to Generation X, and I have lived a full life. I have served in the military, married, had kids, and divorced. Now in my 40s, I wonder: *Is this it?* Is this all life has to offer? This is what I waited all those many years to become: a sarcastic teacher who still has to clip coupons because I pay child support?

So I began to write. I began blogging about 8 years ago, and on average, I have a couple of hundred people a week read them. They started as rough little tid-bits--small half-formed dwarves thrown onto the information superhighway to be picked up, ran over, or ignored. They lacked formal editing or the refined airs of professional publication. Sometimes they were crude. But they were always honest. They are my children, and they are special to me. So I've cleaned them up and repackaged them into a nice little collection. I did this because people ask me, "Why don't you publish these into a book?"

I resisted this at first. For me, blogging was a way to cope with my divorce. They say comedians are miserable individuals. There is some truth in that. I blogged to express my feelings in a positive way—and if people found amusement in them—so much the better. It never occurred to me to publish them. Secondly, we live in a time of internet mob justice. If someone's feelings get hurt, the remedy is to demand the offender's head. Usually that comes in the form of a lost career. In my case, I'm a public school teacher. Most of what I write is offensive. That is why I waited almost a decade to consolidate my blogs into a book. I have a house and two girls to raise. So I kept my blogs limited to a select audience. Then I decided, "Fuck it." I served my country, and I earned my free speech. I don't believe speech should have a codicil that states "terms and conditions may apply." Don't get me wrong; I'm not a Free Speech Activist. I'm just an asshole who's looking to publish a book. And I did, albeit under a pseudonym that separates my thoughts from my real identity.

This is my written history. They are thoughts, and observations as a disaffected member of Generation X. There are no structural constrictions contained here. These are just blogs in no particular order.

And I hope you enjoy them.

And Now Some Parting Gifts…

"Thank you Frank Swanson for playing the game of *Married*. Unfortunately you lost, but our sponsors have provided you with some wonderful parting prizes.

First, we'll present you with **Bad Credit**! Yes, Frank, your wife's inability to pay her bills will make it so that you couldn't charge a 25-cent gumball or lease something more spacious than a box in the ghetto!

Next you'll get a monthly **Child Support Bill!** Your wife's primordial ability to give life birth ensures that you have no disposable income for the next 12 years! Watch in amazement as you are denied seeing the kids and every dime you make doesn't finance your children, but your wife's trailer-set lifestyle! So while you are at home, watching shitty reruns on TV rather than traveling, thank **Child Support** for your poverty.

And just because the marriage ends doesn't mean you ever have to stop listening to her **Mouth!** Imagine a 2,000 horsepower machine that produces enough crap to fertilize a small island. Like the fictional Terminator, **Mouth** has no pity, no remorse, and it will not stop until you are dead!

And pack your bags, we're sending you on a **Guilt Trip!** For the next 12 or more years, you'll spend lounging in the ex-spouse paradise of **Guilt Trip**. All expenses are yours, of course. On your journey, you'll experience cruelty, lies, and outright humiliation from the same person who you once pledged your sacred vows.

And we'll see you next time on *Married!"*

--All I can do is laugh

The $45 Wedding Vow

Through careful analysis, I have discovered the price of wedding vows. They cost $45. That was the amount I got when I pawned my wedding ring today. The funny thing is that I paid over $1,000 for it. I could have taken it to a gold dealer and gotten more for it, but I decided that the amount was a perfect metaphor for how my marriage ended.

Armed with $45, I went out and blew it on booze.

It felt good.

Just Spit Balling Here

Adventures in Dating: The Walking Dead

I don't want to be buried, in a Pet Sem-e-tary.
--The Ramones

As a general rule, I've learned to never date teachers.
Why?

They're all f**king nuts!

The teachers I've dated fall into two general categories;
fascist control freaks or bat-shit-pants-on-your-head crazy.
I've experienced teachers attempt to regulate how I ate, what
I drank, how often I should see them. I've been threatened,
stalked, and hounded. It's a shame there is no support group
for the victims of academia. I can't be the only one.

About two months ago, I broke that vow. I don't know
why I broke it. Perhaps I was bored. Maybe it's because I
knew this teacher was slightly Mansonesque crazy, and I
like to live dangerously. Mind you, I did not rush head long
into this endeavor. I carefully weighed the risks versus the
reward. I figured meeting for a couple of drinks didn't merit
a red alert on the danger scale. My rationale for asking her
out was like the doctor in Pet Semetary when he buried his
cat; if it didn't work out, he could kill it and no one would be
none the wiser. Granted, I couldn't kill HER, but I could kill
the relationship before the roots of psycho took root.

We met at a bar. I like taking girls to bars so I can "water board" them with alcohol and extract every ounce of potential harm they have planned for a potential mate. We were supposed to meet at 8:00. By 8:20 she called and said she was running late. That figures. This is the same teacher who strolls into every faculty meeting 20 minutes late to make her grand appearance....for the past decade.

When she arrived, I bought her a drink and she launched into a monologue about work. This is another reason I hate dating teachers. All they want to talk about is f**king work. "Why doesn't Jimmy learn? Why doesn't the Administration understand my brilliance? This is how I would change education..."

I loathe that shit. By 4:00, I make it a general rule to leave my brain at work where upon my deepest thoughts center around dick and fart jokes. I tried to steer the conversation in other directions, but I failed. She monopolized the conversation so thoroughly, even the guy in the top hat on the Milton Bradley version of the game would have face-palmed.

Her: "This one time when I was in Spain earning my third Master's Degree in Spanish, after the one I got from Trinity University..."

Me: "Speaking of Spain--"

Her: "Then when I was in Peru, a local prince wanted to marry me, then..."

Me: "What other parts of Latin America--"

Her: "I demand excellence from my students. If they can't speak perfect Castilian Spanish after three days of verb conjugations then...."

 Me: "What about---"

Her: "I am convinced the other teachers in my department loathe me because I am white and I speak better Spanish than Queen Isabella..."

Me: *Fuck it. Just let her talk.*

For the next three hours, she droned on and on. It was like a verbal equivalent of the Spanish inquisition. Yes, I felt hostage to her own unique form of social terrorism. I was being drowned in a pool of H-E-R! From this experience affirms Einstein's Theory of Relativity. Time is relative. It is affected by gravity and, most importantly, BOREDOM! By the second hour of my ordeal, I felt every nanosecond drag on. As per the laws of physics, I should have emerged from this date the same age while my daughters had become grandmothers in their own right.

In an attempt to shut her up, I tried to find things I could shove in her mouth to shut her the fuck up without being arrested. Had I had access to an EKG, my boredom could have been measured...literally to death.

Her: "This one time, when I was dating Pablo Escobar, we took a helicopter ride..."

My EKG Reading: Thump, Thump, Thump, Thump

Her: "There was this conspiracy against me at work one time when I acquired a flesh-eating bacteria...."

EKG Reading: Thump....Thump....

Her: "Then when I had this life-or-death case of carpal tunnel syndrome..."

EKG Reading:
Thump............Thump..

Her: "I organize my classes into learning groups where upon...."

EKG Reading: --

I died.

Her monologue literally slayed me.

It's all fun and games until someone dies. My eyes glazed over and I became hungry. I am not sure why I didn't immediately dig into her navel to get a mouthful of intestines. Perhaps a small part of my brain survived in an effort to save humanity. After all, this bitch was the "Typhoid Mary" of the Zombie Apocalypse and I was the unwitting Index case.

For the sake of humankind, will someone please cleanse her with fire? Our fate depends on it!

Adventures in Dating: Sketches of Crazy People

Finding females to date is not hard in San Antonio. Provided you have a job and don't live with your mom, you are a virtual Hugh Hefner. However, me being me, I always attract the most fucked up females in the history of courtship. Here are a few more examples of why I should shoot myself rather than date:

1. 90's Hillary Clinton
*Seriously, I went out with a girl who looked just like Hillary Clinton before alcohol and Benghazi scandals wore her down. It's not that I find Hillary Clinton attractive. I figured it's a title shot so I could brag to my friends in 2016: "Yeah, the President, I totally fucked her."

It is because of this experience why I am leery of dating females in the winter. They wear long sleeves, and can thus hide their deformities. Upon taking her to the bar, she took off her coat and revealed:
...her hairy-ass arms.

It wasn't just regular hair one might find on a Cro-Magnon specimen. This bitch had hair designed to capture plankton in the ocean. It was disgusting. I don't even remember anything she had to say (I know, that is my usual MO with women, but this one even more so). All I could focus on was the hair on her arms. It was like she went into this teleportation chamber and fused with a fly at a molecular level.

Her physical impairment helped shape my political views to this day.

2. Hezbollah

*Yes, I went out with a terrorist. A girl born and raised in Egypt, I dared asked her feelings about current events in the Middle East. It went like this:

Me: "What does the average Egyptian think about Israel?"

Hezbollah Girl: "The Jews agitate everything--"

Me thinking *Please don't do this*

Hezbollah Girl: "The American media is run by Jews"

...and you're doing this

After the usual monologue cliché of Jews-run-the world-so-I'll-don-a-suicide-vest was over, I ended the date and reminded myself why I enlisted in the first place.

3. The Incredible Melting Nurse.

*I went out with this nurse simply because of her name: It was one of those girls who demanded she be called by all three names, and because she was Hispanic, it was really long. I've never been out with someone who had 10 syllables in their name, and the novelty struck me. Oh, I paid for that one.

I will say this. She had big hair; I mean really big hair. Big hair is something the 80s got right. If I could find a chick with a lion's mane I would. Big hair is good. On the minus side...

I took her to a bar and ordered a drink. Upon her first sip she began to sweat profusely. She informed me that booze makes her sweat. She didn't just perspire, she poured water out of her skin. I don't think I am out of line when I say moist women are a turnoff. They can grow mold. I offered to dial 911 but she declined. I seriously thought she might slough off her skin and eat mine to stay alive.

Give me time. I get the winners, and if nothing else-- hilarity will ensue. More to report as I am apparently the Stanley Livingston of jungle dating.

Teacher of the Month

It doesn't matter what school or what part of the country you live in, all faculty meetings follow a specific template meticulously designed not to just waste time, but kill it in the most gruesome way imaginable. Here is how:

Faculty meetings always begin with the ritual of nominating a Teacher of the Month. It's a performance award in the form of a framed certificate--printed earlier that same morning--and given to an educator in front of his or her colleagues. In every other organization in the civilized world, superior performance is awarded with something tangible, like cash. The logic behind a Teacher of the Month award is so insidious, I admire its evil. The Administration figures giving the serfs nothing more than a "somebody likes me" award will keep them quiet on the manor.

And for the most part, they are right.

The winners run down to collect their award like they were selected for participation in the "Price is Right;" their glee a testament to our institutional cheapness. Now, understand something, how is "good will" a commodity? What can one purchase with good will? Can you call a Wall Street broker and invest it?

"Yes, can I purchase 100 shares of IBM on my goodwill credit card?"

No.

Trying to get everyone to like you is not always the wisest course of action. The last person that attempted to make friends with everyone was Jesus--

--and we all know what happened to him.

So who are the typical awardees, you might ask? It's the same 5 assholes who get it every month on a rotating basis. Of course there is the obligatory clapping amongst those teachers who have resigned themselves to the status of Pavlovian hounds. The real celebration comes from those who won the betting pool of "which self-promoting dick got it this month?"

The part I find funny in these awards are the citations themselves. The Principal recites their acts of educational valor as though they were being awarded a silver star. The phrases used are hilarious:

 "For putting in long hours..."

*By this logic, working deserves an award? Do they think it's like this:

Me, tied to a whipping post as the Field Manager admonishes me

"What's your name?!" He screams.

"Kunta Kente"

Whip cracks

"Toby," he screams. "Your name is Toby!"

"Spends a lot of time ensuring student success..."

*That implies the rest of us slouches burn through our days off by early September and are compelled to nurse our hang-overs with videos in the morning until we are well enough to surf the internet.

"Exhibits a positive attitude"
Well, if that is a criteria for the coveted Teacher of the Month, it pretty much eliminates the social studies and art teachers.

What is really funny is Teacher of the Month can be anyone on staff, not necessarily a teacher. One month our Librarian got it. No shit. The one person whose whole career has been replaced with a Google search engine actually won. Like the Luddites of old, this woman spent her whole career railing against modern informational access:

"Wikipedia is the Devil!"

"Really, the Dewy Decimal System is valid!"

I would not be surprised if she actually threw a wooden shoe into the server to burn the system down.

I do not know how to win the coveted "Teacher of the Month" award. After 16 years, I have resigned myself to the fact it is better to mock the unattainable.

Useless Jobs

In these lean economic times, jobs are at a premium. If I were President Obama, I think I might help the economy by trimming the fat from our country, and creating jobs that are actually useful. We waste so much money subsidizing useless careers that our economy would be better served by making the following jobs illegal:

1. High School Football Coach. These assholes make in excess of $70,000 a year for their ability to pit the enemies of X and O in battle. X and O are in an eternal struggle for supremacy from the battlefields of tic-tac-toe to "school-boy football" play offs. In reality, X and O will never resolve their differences and we, taxpayers, should not be forced to fund unending wars.

2. Any Employee of the Department of Indian Affairs. Uhh, Geronimo died a long time ago. The Ghost Dance War of 1905 ended…in 190-fucking-5! Indians don't bother us anymore. They run casinos and sell cheap cigarettes. I do not see any need for Indian Affairs Agents to be employed anymore.

3. Librarians. Wow, I learned about the Dewy-Decimal System as a 15 year old freshman. Librarians got a Masters Degree in a filing system that is now obsolete with the advent of Wikipedia….and yet, they make the same money I do. In essence, they have become more learned janitors than anything else. When the last time you saw a librarian do anything more useful other than push in a chair or shelve a book? Employees of Barnes and Nobles shelve books for $7 an hour.

4. Journalist. Telling lies is bad. Yet, they do it for a living.

5. Chiropractor. These are modern day witch doctors armed with one anatomy course with sprinklings of voodoo. Every professional chiropractor is a failed medical student. They are little more than message therapists minus the happy ending.

6. Acupuncture Professionals. Mating the noun acupuncture with professional is like linking the words military intelligence; a cliché that serves a greater lie. This ancient Asian medical practice is akin to cutting holes in your skull to let the evil spirits out. How many diseases has acupuncture cured? The correct answer is zero. Let's break this down, shall we?
Acupuncture vs. Cancer: Cancer wins
Acupuncture vs. Arthritis: Arthritis wins
Acupuncture vs. Polio: Polio wins

Personally, I think Acupuncture professionals should team up with Chiropractors and Fortune Tellers and make a wellness clinic where they could more effectively service the dumb!

7. Dietician. These assholes went to 4 years of college and learned one thing; eat less, lose weight. I thought that was common sense; but I must be wrong. How does one earn a Masters Degree of Dietician Studies? What are the topics? I can only imagine:

"Put the Donut Down!"

"50 Hot Dogs a Day Allows Diabetes its Way!"

8. Geologist. These people pissed their education away by studying rocks. As a teacher, I teach rocks—yet didn't have to major in them. Geologists have a reputation for being the most overpaid, underwhelming person at any party:

Male Geology Major at a party: "Hey baby, nice to meet ya! Did you know that obsidian rock is actually glass?"
 Female: "Nice story dude. I am going back to my friends now, okay?"

Frank Swanson

Curious Porn Titles

I find when I am down, I'll do something stupid to amuse myself. To keep abreast of the latest porn trends, I decided to Google porn film titles. I don't actually watch porn; as a matter of fact, I find it boring. I think it's like watching animal planet, sans fur and snouts. What boggles me is the process of titling these 90 minute celluloid sins. I am curious as to the logic, or lack of it. I know they want to make money, as the production costs of using the director's bedroom and top quality stars from the local methadone clinic must set them back a few dozen dollars. To recoup this investment, they frequently title them after real Hollywood movies. Sometimes they are clever, but most of the time they sound as though they were named by a pervert with Turrets Syndrome. Here are some real life titles, complete with "how they fail analysis:"

1. Riding Miss Daisy. This one very disturbing. Its namesake was a story about a chauffeur and rich woman developing a relationship in their golden years. I imagine this film attempts to parody the original with images of octogenarian intercourse. I find this as vulgar and sexually repulsive as any episode of the Golden Girls where Rhue McClallehan cracked joke after dick-shrinking joke about her sex life.

2. Fatal Erection. This doesn't sound like porn at all. It sounds like a warning for the side effects of Viagra. "Tell your doctor about an erection lasting more than four hours as it can be a fatal erection." I'm not a doctor, but I am reasonably sure erections are not life threatening. Even if they were, how does one treat a fatal erection? I know, make them watch an hour of Golden Girls. That'll cure it—forever. Perhaps Fatal Erection can be a double feature with the memorable hit, Die Hard-On.

3. Don't Say A Word, My Parents Are Home. Is this legal to watch? Or will one download it, only to have FBI agents crash through the door, catching the offender with his pants around his ankles and a surprised look?

4. Sorest Rump. A porn based on a character with mental disabilities. I will forgo the tidal wave of tasteless jokes begging to be written. It just bothers me to think that characters like Rain Man, Sling Blade, and Forrest Gump do…THAT! They are cute, and until now, incorruptible.

5. Jesus Christ, Porn Star. Everyone who toiled on this movie, from director and stars to the guy mopping the floor up will all have one thing in common; they can brag to all their friends in Hell they were part of this movie. There is absolutely no redemption for anyone involved in this piece of shit in Christian theology. I checked.

6. Glad He Ate Her. Porn might not be for everybody, but you gotta hand it to the producers; they try to capture as much of the market as possible. In this case, they are targeting the Jeffrey Dahmer and Ed Gein consumers. Nothing can warm the ole tender feelings faster than carnal delights followed up with cannibalism and skin wearing!

7. Angry Gay Men. Funny someone would make fictional porn after real life. Most of us would call that a documentary, and Angry Gay Men could have been filmed in Prison. Yikes, watch out for the soap!

8. Raging Butt. This crosses any line of decency or taste. A raging butt is a biological reaction, and hardly a carnal delight. One encounters a raging butt the morning after a long night of chili dogs and beer. Now I know who filmed "Two Girls, One Cup."

9. Malcom XXX. Mmm, take civil rights leaders and diminish and their accomplishments by mocking them in a porn. This doesn't sound like entertainment to me. It rings more of Klan propaganda. Perhaps their next block buster will be "The Adventures of Martin Labia King."

10. Lord of the G Strings. Ways to mock Saxon literature yet, at the same time, add some entertainment to the Lord of the Rings. I believe watching dwarfs copulate must be infinitely more entertaining than watching them walk in a haunted forest for 3 hours.

The Top 10 Things You Should Never Say!

Through painstaking research and life experience, I've learned there are things you never say, no matter the circumstances. Naturally, I learned the hard way…

10. "No thanks, I've had enough."
9. "I can't. I'm married."
8. "Yeah, Drill Sergeant, when I get around to it."
7. "No, no. It's not contagious until it flares up."
6. "Are those real?"
5. "Oh c'mon officer! I can't even walk a straight line when I'm sober!"
4. "I swear to protect and defend the Constitution of the United States"
3. Sure mom, I'd like to hear your opinion on the matter."
2. "You're right, the whole thing's a mess, and it's my fault."
1. "I do.

Frank Swanson

Teaching Sucks

If you ever get a chance to teach.... don't. You'd do better to masturbate for cash.

Last week, the Texas Legislature voted to cut our $800 pay raise by 50%.

Is it just me or did they actually have the balls to cut an ***800 dollar a year raise by HALF!*** Let's break down this massive chunk of change that I'll be putting in my pocket by the next fiscal year. Half of 800 is 400 (see, and I am a graduate of public high school!). You take 400 and divide it by 12. You make an approximate $33 a month before taxes. After you tack on my tax burden, my take home "raise" from a generous Texas legislature is about 15 dollars.

Thanks guys, I'll try not to spend it all in one place.

In a state that drowns in oil with an inflationary curve that generates more money than I can count, I ask why? It's not like any of those funds went to upgrade our electrical grid. It's been providing semi-reliable energy since its construction back in 1872. It's only killed 700 people in one freeze, so its working as intended. Maybe it went to the police. I'm not sure about that. All Texas police agencies have tanks and more than enough gear to grind down minority communities. For the most part, all that gear barely goes used. Ask Uvalde Police Department. They'd rather

22

listen to children die than get a scratch on their brand-new armored vehicle.

They have the money to pay teachers, but they won't. It's easier to watch public education whither on the vine so public tax dollars can flow to churches where "Dinosaur-as-theory" is being taught. And that is what they will get as a work force—a pack of cretins who fear science because they don't understand anything that wasn't white-washed through an evangelical lens.

I hate this state.

Frank Swanson

Adventures in Dating: Tinder-Normal Activity

I am a victim of terrorism, and this is my story…

I'm not much into online dating, as I prefer to fail in person. However, Tinder appeals to my shallowness. You girl shop by swiping right to like and left to discard. This is my experience on the app.

Nope

Nope

Nope

Obvious Bot

Nope

Way-out-of-my-league, but I'll try anyway

Obvious Bot

Bingo! Normal person.

So last week I matched with a girl, and we eventually started texting. According to her profile, she was pretty, employed, had all of her teeth, and not addicted to narcotics. Hey, that already makes her better than my ex-wife. How bad can it be, right?

 Then reality hit me harder than a Bill Cosby cocktail.

 Upon walking into the bar, I was captured and held captive by a social terrorist. You see, she looked NOTHING like her picture. What awaited me was a human tank; a big giant monster perched on a stressed barstool. The bitch did the ole, "angle picture" that cleverly hid 1,247 pounds of her. She even managed to photo-shop a chin. She didn't carry just a few extra pounds; she was "how much for Han

Solo" fat. It's the oldest trick in the book, and I fell victim to it. Don't get me wrong. I have dated plus sized women before, and they were beautiful. I have no problem with that. This one f**king lied to me; and that's the source of my rage.

In our discourse, I indicated that I'm active. In the unspoken dating code that means I'm in shape and I expect a little reciprocity. But in her world, I suppose she took that to mean:

"Well, round is a shape. So yeah, I'm in shape too."

She even claimed to scuba dive. Physics says: "That is a lie." She further deceived me by telling me how much she liked to hike in state and national parks. That's bullshit, and I know it. There haven't been any documented cases of Sasquatch sightings in Texas.

So I resigned myself to spending the next couple of hours held captive by Al-Caloria. In a hostage situation, it's best to find refuge in your mind. So I played a game:
Who's here with the fattest girl?

--I f**king won.

I excused myself several times to use the bathroom. Once safe from her carnivorous glare, I texted several of my friends—actually composing this blog while held hostage. Here are a few:

Me: "She's bigger than the tracked vehicles I operated in the military."

Friend 1: "Does she have a nice demeanor?"

Me: "I don't know. I stopped paying attention an hour ago."

Friend 2: "Don't be mean."

Me: "I'm mean? No. The Pillsbury tank girl is mean by

lying to me. It's sad when I can't tell her apart from my SUV."

After a couple of hours, I escaped Sasquatch's big, meaty claws. Some of you might be sympathetic to the terrorist. And yes, I understand the psychological trap of Stockholm Syndrome too. But don't lose sight of the fact that I am the real victim here. And if victims of social terror don't speak up, then….

The terrorists will win.

Soup

I have discovered that selecting the right kind of soup to fit your tastes induces hypertension. There seem to be endless varieties of soup to purchase, yet, upon closer inspection; one discovers the Campbell's quagmire of lies and vomitous tastes.

All I wanted was a beef and vegetable soup. My needs were simple. I was too tired to make a real meal, and--as a bachelor--real meals are hard to come by. I looked at the labels to see what morsels each can contained. Every one of 100 varieties of beef and vegetable soup, had one disgusting vegetable that I wouldn't put in my mouth. One boasted of having peas. Gross! Peas possess the texture and taste of warm boogers. Another contained mushroom. A fungus. I don't like fungus on my feet, much less in my mouth. Another had something called lentil. The picture of the contents looked like a regular beef and vegetable soup mixed with tiny little maggots floating around. One soup was unique in that it had lima beans. Lima beans? Aren't those canned vegetables that one donates to the poor at school every Christmas season? One soup prided itself with black-eyed peas. In the Northern United States, black eyed peas are fed to hogs. In the Southern United States, black eyed peas are consumed by white trash too poor to afford navy beans. They taste like dirt. Every New Years, my mother attempts to make me consume one spoon of black eyed peas so that my New Year's wishes will be fulfilled. This is how that worked out.

Frank Swanson

The year was New Years 2006:

*As I consumed my spoonful of black eyed peas to appease
the New Years Wish God:*

*"Wow, these taste like shit! I wish for a new year with
humble aspirations. I celebrate my drug-free, loyal wife, my
adoring step-daughter who loves me as her father, and my
wonderful two story home."*

Instead, I lost the house, my cunt of an ex-wife shoved
more chemicals in her face than a pharmaceutical company,
and my lovely step-daughter ran away. I am convinced ***it's
because*** I ate those fucking black eyed peas. So, needless to
say, I do not consume black eyed peas.

"Fuck it." I live in south Texas, I'll eat a taco instead.

Demonology 101

Today I watched both the Exorcist and the Exorcism of Emily Rose, classic masterpieces about demonic possession. Both are based on true stories, and they scare the shit out of me. I've made some observations about them..

First of all, who are the people who get possessed? Little girls, so I guess I'm safe. Reagan was possessed by Pazuzu for playing "Light as a Feather, Stiff as a Board," while Emily Rose was possessed because God just hated her. I know some people at work who I wished would get possessed; it would do wonders for their personality.

Second of all, let's explore the nature of the demons that do the possessing. They represent sin incarnate. Think about that. They are sin. Drinking is a sin. So is pre-marital sex. The last I checked, my music collection contains some very sinful lyrics. So why do the demons do fucked-up shit to their victims? I mean wouldn't it be different to get possessed by a demon who wants to go bar hopping, while grooving to Rob Zombie? And still hook up at the end of the night? That would make sense. But no. That doesn't happen. Instead, the possessed lay around in bed, puking green shit, and chatting in Aramaic. You would figure that the demons would seize the opportunity of leaving hell the way we would a vacation. Instead, they bring their work with them. That would be like me going to London and making lesson plans. Loosen up guys! When you're off the clock, you can relax a little. Not all sin has to be so vulgar. For instance, you can sin by masturbating. It's wicked and entertaining. Masturbating demons have a bonus that comes with possessed pocket-pool; it causes blindness! What I'm saying is demons can break some Commandments **and** still have a good time.

And finally, who wrote the book on Exorcism? Can we really trust the Roman Ritual? It killed two priests in the Exorcist and imprisoned one in the Exorcism of Emily Rose. Knowing that, if I were a priest, I wouldn't be inclined to perform Exorcisms. I wouldn't care if the victim were speaking backwards lyrics found in an Ozzy Osborne album. Fuck that! I figure better to live and bless another day than risk life and freedom for some poor schmuck who serves as an infernal joyride. Better her than me. I'd most likely refer the possessed to a mental retardation home. I hear that they're real snazzy here in Texas!

T.V. From the 70s and 80s

I have a lot of time on my hands of late which I diligently use to philoso-fize themes in life while watching reruns of programs I watched as a kid. As an educated adult watching TV shows that amused me in my youth, I came to a hard realization:

I must be fucking stupid!

That, or the Hollywood moguls that churned out the crap Americans watched in the 70s, believed all of us were mentally handicapped. Let's break down some of these popular 70's TV shows.

1. **The A-Team**. Military fugitives who travel around in a "child molester van" save the day from criminals whose corruption escapes regular law enforcement agencies. The victims that usually hire the A-Team are white-trash types which leaves me wondering; *How in the fuck can they afford to pay for the services of an entire A-Team when Blackwater Inc pays $200,000 a year per special forces soldier?*

This now leads me to question the military aspects of the A-Team. Having been a former military man, I have a basic understanding of how Special Forces operate. First of all, an A-Team is comprised of 12 men. Not the 5 sported in the show. Each has a specialty. For instance, there is a weapons MOS, a medical MOS, and an Engineer MOS. But in the TV A-Team there is a guy known only as "Face." I am not real sure if there is an MOS known as "Face" or how that would be useful in Special Operations warfare. Perhaps a "Face-Man" is the guy who takes one for the team by being sodomized for information. That is one job the Army leaves out of its commercials, and for good reason! Imagine this:

Army Strong! Rectally speaking, of course!

The last 15 minutes of any A-Team show has the same hare-brained scheme that any Special Olympiad could foil given half a chance. Usually the A-Team constructs an "improvised weapon" which disperses lettuce heads at an enemy while thousands of AK-47 rounds are spewing wantonly in the air. And yet there are no fatalities! Perhaps that is why we won the Cold War; Russian-made weapons don't actually hurt anyone! Well, unless you had a lettuce cannon accompanying it.

2. **The Golden Girls**. Of all the media that influences us to have sex, the Golden Girls was the first show to actually turn us against it. Unless you are Norman Bates, then a bunch of blue-haired old ladies bragging on their sexcapades should have repulsed any normal human being. What kind of sexual masochist would tune in for such torture? What is the opposite of a pedophile? An Octogenarian-O-File? Yuck! I don't find the idea of gray, caved in vaginas appealing. If I ever get serious about priest-hood, I'll tune into the Golden Girls!

3. The Rockford Files.   Let me get this straight. A former convict who lives in a trailer can outwit the by solving crimes that professional forensic scientists can't. He is a former con for a reason; he was nabbed by the same dimwits that can't solve a crime without him. Did James Rockford commit his crime in front of the jury? Is that why he is a convict?

4. Logan's Run. A classic post-apocalyptic thriller where population growth is kept in check by executing people on their 30th birthday. As a kid watching this, I thought it was quite reasonable that anyone over 30 was useless and worthy of execution. Why all the fuss? Why should anyone in their right mind identify with an aged old fart who wanted to flee his fate? As an adult, I've decided…not so much.

5. Land of the Lost This "ass-terpiece" is the reason why I flunked both biology and geology. A family goes kayaking down a river only to find themselves inexplicably lost in the Jurassic Age where rubbery dinosaurs and plastic-suited "Sleesticks" threaten to eat them every week.

6. Sanford and Son. Oh yes, this show does wonders for race relations in America. Black people are wise hermits that live in junkyards. The only white character is the bumbling cop who couldn't solve a crime without Fred Sanford.

Frank Swanson

A Few Thoughts About JFK...

I visited Dallas over Spring Break. I had to see where JFK used his head to catch bullets.

Anyway, I am not going to write about him or the assassination. We all know the CIA was behind it. What I need to address is how lame a site it was, and how I could spice it up were I in charge of things!

First of all, you pay 10 dollars to go to the 6th floor where Oswald "shot" Kennedy. You enter the elevators, surrounded by drooling idiots learning there was a JFK in the first place. When the elevator doors open, the visitor is surrounded by pictures and models of that afternoon back in 1963. Quickly, I skipped to the place Oswald "took the shot" and found the whole thing encased in glass.

How lame.

Boxes in glass. No rifles, no spent shells. Just boxes.

The rest of the museum is a fairy tale denying physics and common sense in light of the film footage. Oh well, so much for accuracy.

After a 15 minute waste of time, I ventured down to the gift store looking for something cool to buy. There was nothing that interested me. So, it set me to thinking about how I would jazz the place up a bit.

First, I would let people actually step into Lee Harvey Oswald's space when he "shot" Kennedy. I would even have a replica of the rifle mounted to a video game where you could "peer outside" and shoot at the President as he rolled by. I'd even program it so that you could even pop Jackie O's ass. Extra points would be given for accuracy and speed. It would be like "Call of Duty, Oswald Edition."

Next, the gift shop *has* to be brought up to date. I'd sell merchandise that make one realize they were at an assassination place. Here are a few items I would like marketed:

Games

Operation: JFK Edition: It would be just like the old game, but in this one, the object is to remove pieces of shrapnel from JFK's head. Careful not to touch the sides or the President's nose turns red and buzzes!

Warren Commission Game of Bullshit: 4 to 6 players sit around a table and pass off the biggest whoppers until challenged by someone who screams, "Bullshit!"

Accessories:

JFK Piggy Bank! Store loose change in a replica of the president's head. When you're ready to collect, simply take it out the range and shoot it! Fun for all ages!

T-Shirt: With a picture of JFK saying something to the effect of: "I went to Dallas and all I brought back was a gaping hole in my head!"

JFK Joke book: Filled with crowd pleasers like, "Why did JFK cross the road? To get to his head on the other side!"

Yeah, I think that would about do it.

Just Spit Balling Here

A Few Thoughts on Star Wars

After having been a Star Wars freak for almost 30 years, there are some things I'd like to point out about the 2 trilogies that have perplexed me:

On Luke and Leia

The twins were separated at birth to prevent Darth Vader from discovering and killing them. Leia went on to live in a plush palace on the paradise planet of Alderan. There, she lived a life of luxury and was educated at the finest schools.

Luke was left with some hillbillies on the ass-end of the universe; the dustbowl that is Tatooine. There, he farmed with his hick aunt and uncle who gave him crap every time he wanted power converters. We know he had no education since Uncle Owen chained him to the farm. This turned Luke into one Meth habit away from full-blown Bumpkin.

I bet there was some serious sibling rivalry issues both dealt with in later years.

Imperial Military Career

Advancement is the goal of every military officer be it in the United States or in the Imperial Galactic Navy. However, since Darth Vader has a habit of "Force-strangling" any flag officer that pissed him off, am I to believe that the best of the Imperial Navy avoided advancement? The desire to survive outweighs anything else, so I imagine that the bright officers sought out of the way duty stations or placement in the supply corps. The only ones left in the combat arms branch of the Imperial Navy were the dolts. Is that why the Rebel Alliance managed to survive? Was it due to idiocy on behalf of the Imperial Staff officers? I think so, or else the rebel alliance would have died on Hoth.

Speaking of the Rebel Alliance

I never really liked them. I look at the Empire and I see uniformity and military order. They can engage an enemy under any conditions. The rebel alliance, on the other hand, is a potpourri of misfits from all over the galaxy. They use Squids as admirals, chicks as Special Forces, and their equipment is second rate. I look at the Rebels and see militant hippies and galactic environmentalists. Seriously...they won? It was the faulty chain of command in the Imperial Navy that led to the victory at the Battle of Endor.

Darth Vader, a Chump!

After having reviewed all 6 movies I've come to the conclusion that Darth Vader wasn't the big deal that the prophecy predicted.

Darth Vader got his ass kicked by Count Dooku, Obi Wan Kenobi, and his own son, Luke. With a record like that, it makes France look good at war.

Obi Wan Kenobi was a far superior Jedi. He beat Darth Maul, General Grievious, and Darth Vader the first time. The only reason he lost to Darth Vader the second time was that he was so old that he farted dust. It would be like me boxing my beloved grand-father who is in his eighties.

Frank Swanson

I Am Caveman, Hear Me Roar!

I have found a new direction to take my life. I am going
to evolve into a caveman. I've even named my new species
Hetro-Erectus. It is a procreation variant of the ancestor
species, Homo Erectus whose bones are well preserved in
the San Francisco Bay Area.

So why would anyone in their right mind *want* to be a
caveman? Well, I like the outdoors and life for cavemen
was an eternal camp trip. Even when they sought refuge in a
shitty, drafty hole a mountain, it's still plusher than my
apartment.

Cavemen possessed the one attribute that many of us
lack: honesty. Back in the day, if someone annoyed a
caveman, nature's law dictated the offending party's
immediate execution. With the advent of laws and
government, the annoying behavior gene flourished, thus
allowing people like my ex-wife a survival opportunity that
wouldn't be afforded her.

Does anyone ever see Cavemen in strip bars? Of course
not, because their chicks run around naked all the time. That
saves them a lot of money both on lap dances and drug
habits. I kinda dig Cave chicks. They have big hair like the
80s. I like big hair.

You never see cavemen punching a time card at a job
they hate. What did they do? Eat and fuck. It's kinda like
me in the summer--minus the saber tooth tigers. If the

person who invented work lived back in caveman days, his immediate execution would have been followed with ritual cannibalism.

I know what you might be thinking. *Cavemen didn't have the internet. Where would we access porn?* Cavemen did have an early version of internet porn. We call it cave painting. It was sort of a Paleolithic information early pathway. There we can see Grog boning Bree just like the antelopes in the savannahs below. Except the antelopes didn't have a comic bubble saying, "Fuck me harder Grog! Give it to me like a...like a...like a CAVEMAN!" Besides, they resided in communal areas. While the rest of us have to travel to Mexico for free sex shows, cavemen got it right in their own homes!

Ahh, a caveman's life is the life for me!

Frank Swanson

Terror at 30,000 Feet!

What many travel consultants fail to mention in preparing
a voyage, is that it is wise to allot time for the bathroom
prior to boarding a plane. I learned this one the hard way.

What follows is a tale of gripping fear and terror that
only the brave need read further.

I woke up late the day I almost died. My plane was due
to leave in an hour, and my friends scrambled to brew
coffee, and ensure I got off safely. Nolan checked my bags,
and Sarah poured me a cup of Joe to shake off last night's
booze. We piled into the car and we made it to the airport
with 30 minutes to spare. Just enough time to check my
bags, strip-search, and get to my seat. As I passed through
airport security, it happened.

I had to shit.

There was no time for a dreaded public bathroom dump,
so I board the plane and strapped in. The belt squeezed my
belly, further aggravating the boiling tar baby waiting for
birth. The plane pressurized and I went into contractions.
Not too bad at first, they were 10 minutes apart, so I had
time. The idea of shitting in the plane was a no-go. Not
only do I have this irrational fear of the bathroom falling off
the plane while I'm inside relieving myself, I'm afraid my
noxious vapors might leak out into the cabin, killing the last

four rows of passengers. I don't need to spend time at Guantanamo just for dropping kids off at the pool.

Okay, the plane flight is about two hours. I thought I could handle that.

How wrong I was.

The fury of processed steak, pizza, and chips painfully swirled about in a belly full of last night's beer. It screamed for birth. A chance at life. As the first hour rolled into the second, I feared I might be pregnant with something monstrous, like in that movie, Alien. It punched at my bowels, threatening to tear through my flesh only to wreak havoc on passengers and crew. I felt a tinge of guilt as I am the mother of this hideous monster.

I braved the pain. The only thing keeping it inside and me is the hour layover in Dallas where even the filthiest of bathrooms would have been an oasis of relief. We landed, and right before rolling to the gate, we stopped. In the middle of the runway. Fifty feet from the gate and the heavenly relief of a functional toilet. Or non-functional. I didn't care.

The Captain's voice came over the speaker. "Wha Wha Wha...it seems that we have to wait until the other plane clears the gate. It shouldn't be too long, maybe ten to fifteen minutes..."

Ten to Fifteen minutes! Really?! I thrashed about in my seat as the monster inside of me fought for life. My belly swelled as the monster gained strength and fury.

Fifteen minutes stretched into thirty, and I realized I would have to run across Dallas Fort Worth International Airport just to make my connection home. Perhaps that doesn't sound menacing, but a pregnant man in labor sprinting across an airport was the situation I found myself in. But the fun was only beginning.

I found myself in the very back of the plane which meant that I had to wait while all 150 passengers gingerly took their times to collect their bags and meander off the plane. Hate replaced guilt, and I thought about releasing my beast to devour them on the spot. Didn't they know I could have allowed this beast to consume them somewhere over Kansas? Now their dawdling mocked my pain!

I ran to my connection, and almost missed it. By then the pain was so intense and white hot that all I could think was *Shit! Shit! Shit! SHIT!*

Another hour airborne. The pain caused me to black out. The beast inside grew. It was hungry, ready to claim its rightful place among the living. It was ready to hunt. It was ready to kill!

In San Antonio, I finally made it back to my apartment. My pants were at my ankles faster than even the most prolific of porn stars. I jumped on my waiting toilet and squeezed. I remembered my La Maz training as the beast burst through my puckered starfish. I heard it birth growls. It thrashed about in the toilet, searching for prey. Its brotherly toxic fumes pierced my nostrils with such raw power that I relied on my military training to keep awake during this hellish birth.   But even that failed me. The lights spun wildly, and I blacked out.

When I awoke some time later, I found my apartment door ajar and a trail of excrement marking the path my monster left as he prepared to prey on an unsuspecting world.

Frank Swanson

Adventures in Dating: What Women Think

Ok, I know a lot of you are thinking, "Whoah, wait a minute—has Frank actually taken time to explore what a woman thinks?"
To that I can say, hell no! I am two daughters shy of developing full-blown misogyny. However, I have never dated a girl long enough after my divorce to ask for a critique, but I can imagine it would look something like this:
Instance One:
Her: "Hey, I am up here," as she points to her least attractive asset, her face.
Instance Two:
Her: "No, I do not want to hear about how long it took to kill the Lich King in World of Warcraft."
Instance Three
Her: "Are you even listening to me?"
Me: "Well….no. Not really."
So who do I turn to commiserate in the dating wilderness? My ex wife. Yeah I gripe about her frequently, but believe it or not, we get along very well. As a matter of fact, if she had opted for the full personality transplant I encouraged her to get, we'd still be married today. My only concern is that they behave themselves around my daughters. I watch a LOT of Discovery ID. Do the math.
Just saying…

So she tells me about this one, I have to name King of the Douche Bags. Mind you, I did inform her that anything she told me could—and probably would-- be used against her in a blog, but she waived those rights. His name was Kurt. She also begged me not to tag her in this post as she is still Facebook friends with him. I'm still struggling with that one:

Trying not to tag for comedic value if he reads this….trying NOT to be an asshole……hard to resist….
After both she and—more my daughters—relate how douchey this guy was, I looked him up on Facebook. Get this: He said he worked as a "Building Engineer"
A Building Engineer? What in the hell does that mean? Then it struck me. He is prettying up his real job to sound important. In essence, a building engineer is a nice way of saying janitor. That is 2 syllables of BOLD FACED LIE.
Look Scotty, buildings in the 21st Century don't run on Dylithium Crystals, and no one has ever said, "Push the broom faster in the next two minutes or we're all dead!"
This makes me wonder. Can I play this game of dolling up my job to impress the ladies? Let's see, I teach these days, so does that make me an "Information Transfer Specialist.?"
Or better yet, since learning requires the firing of synapses in the brain, can I call myself a neurologist?
So I look at his profile pictures and all I can think of is what my daughters named him:
Sid—from Ice Age. You know, that sloth-looking creature that chases an acorn around glaciers.
Seriously, this guy was all nose and teeth. The trifecta of those features was so large they formed their own gravitational field that focused into a singularity that seemed to be devouring the rest of his face. Did this make him King of the Douche Bags?

No.
Deformed people deserve a little love too.
By night, this janitor is a rock star to the 35 people who show up for the cheap drinks at whatever urine-soaked venue he happens to be playing. While he doesn't take his day job exchanging urinal cakes serious, he believes he is a low rent Eddie Vedder by night. He has 500 pictures of himself holding a guitar. I can't complain about that. Exchange a guitar for guns, and I am just as douchey.
So what defines him as King of the Douche Bags? Well, believing he tripped and fell out of a Star Trek movie is a good start.
Then came Cindy's birthday.
What is the one thing you want to give a new girlfriend for her birthday? Well, if you're Sid, the best gift can only be a framed and autographed picture of YOURSELF! Yes, this cheapskate actually printed an 8X10 picture of himself for her birthday. It must have set him back a whole $2.
I can only imagine how this went down:
"Happy Birthday Hon. I got you the best gift ever. A picture of me!"
Cindy: "Uhh thanks, Dude."
Never once have I thought to give a new girl a picture of myself. Maybe I have thought about this the wrong way. Perhaps there is something to that…
When Cindy and chatted about this, she told me Sid was her first boyfriend when she grew up in Odessa.
Me: "You seriously needed a 12 Step Program."

Cindy: "I didn't drink back then."
Me: "Then you should have."

Just Spit Balling Here

I Suppose this is One Way to Go to Hell!

Al Queda has imagined something so devilishly evil that I am jealous. Just when you think there can't be anything more devious and imaginative, someone always comes about to prove you wrong. Iraqi terrorists once strapped suicide vests onto a couple of retards and detonated them at a Pet Store in Baghdad.

Let's take a minute and review this operation from a logistical standpoint, shall we?

First, while I realize times are hard for terrorists these days, who in the FUCK thought that one up? Did it go something like this?

The scene is a rundown house on the outskirts of Baghdad. Terrorists are sitting around the table thinking of terrorist shit

"Life is hard these days since the surge."

"True that, Achmed. Why just last week those Yankee Imperialist Dogs killed Mohammed!"

"Your cousin, Mohammed?"

"No, the other one."

"Your brother Mohammed?"

"No, not that one either."

"Your nephew Mohammed?"

"Try again."

"Oh, your friend Mohammed."

"Yes. The third one!"

"Yes, I agree. Be brave, Mohammed. Once our ally Hillary Clinton takes over the United States, they will surrender to us!"

"What to do in the meantime..."

All adjust turbans and ponder
"I have it!"
"What is it, Achmed!"
"Do you know my retarded cousin also named Mohammed?"
"Which one?"
"The second one."
"Oh, that Mohammed."
"How about we strap a bomber vest to him and get him to blow himself up!"
"You sure Mohammed is up to the task? How about Mikey? He'll do it. He'll try anything!"
A motherly voice calls from the other room
"Boys, what are you doing?"
Both answer: "Nothing mom!"
"Mohammed is here. I'm sending him in. You play nice now!"
Enter Mohammed (the retarded one), sporting a beanie with a propeller on top and a high water man-dress
"Hello, Achmed and Mohammed! I like peanut butter and jungle gyms."
"Is that so, Mohammed."
"Yes! Momma always says that stupid is as stupid does."
"Try this vest on."
"Is this my magic vest? It matches my magic shoes."
"Why yes, Mohammed. It comes with a button. And when you go to the pet store today to pick up camel crap for dinner tonight, you push it."
"What does it do? Can it make me fly like my Daddy's flying rug? He flies to work every day. He is a city worker. I've always wanted a flying rug of my own, but my Momma

says that special people can't fly rugs, although I don't believe them. But when I get smart enough, I want to live in a bottle."

"Shut up, Mohammed!"

"Okay. But I still want a flying rug."

"Enough!"

"Okay. And a bottle."

"This vest isn't about flying rugs or bottles."

"What does it do then?"

"Well...when you push the button, you get as much peanut butter as you would ever want."

"That sounds great! I'll do it."

Frank Swanson

Adventures in Dating: Funniest Date Ever!

I hate first dates. Oftentimes, the real fiction is not in the movie a couple sees, but in the conversation they share. You have two people suppressing just how crazy they are, hoping their inherent insanity will slowly leak out like a dying balloon so that by the time all of it is out, the other person barely notices. Some are better at hiding than others. Most girls I date just pop their balloon of insanity, and I am left covered in their crazy sauce.

Last night was different.

I met this girl, and we set a date to grab a drink. I like taking girls to drink--not for nefarious reasons, but simply to lube up the truth machine and reveal who they are as people. It has worked in the past and here are some examples:

Psycho #1: "My privates don't work so I use a gel."

Me: *Why are you telling me this on a first date?*

Psycho #2: "I'm married and my husband likes to watch"

Me: *Rome fell in 476 AD. I believe the reason for it was the Roman army was engaged in orgies while Visigoths plundered the city. I will not contribute to a civilization's downfall.*

But I digress. The plan was to meet at the Angry Elephant for a drink. Then she texted me to pick her up because she had been involved in an automobile accident. No problem, I think; everyone has a bad day. If anything, I was impressed she didn't blow off the date. As I leave to pick her up, she calls and asks me to pick her up from her friend's house instead.

That is when my Spidey-too-much-Discovery-ID-Channel-sense goes off. My mind races through a nightmare list of scenarios and settles on the worst one:

*What if her friend is, in fact, 4 giant thugs just paroled, and she is baiting me into a trap. *

So who do I call to ensure my safety? The ex wife. I hate putting my head in my ass in front of her, but the alternative was too nightmarish to risk. It's not like she gives a rat's ass if I live or die as a person. Her interest in my continued health is purely financial. If I die, no more checks. It keeps her honest, and I can respect that.

I explain the situation. "Hey look," I say, "If I don't text you within an hour, can you call the cops? I have a gun, but you never know--"

Then it struck me. I am showing up for a date with a gun tucked in my back pocket. Add a roll of duct tape, a shovel, and I am John Wayne Gacey. I resolved to stop watching Discovery ID at that moment.

So I pick her up, and I am very impressed with the fact she had not had time to get ready because of the car wreck. She apologized for appearance, and I have no idea why. She was beautiful. I deftly throw the gun into the trunk of the car, and we go back to her place where she can get ready. The honesty impressed me:

Girl: 1 Failure: 0

After she readied herself, we drive to the bar. Along the way, I learn she hates Obama, is gainfully employed, does not live with her parents, and likes imported beer.

Girl: 5 Failure: 0

At the bar, we met the most bizarre trio in the history of random meetings. It was a married couple with the ex-wife. How awkward could that be? Well, they reveled in social awkwardness by directing it at us. They pressed us with uncomfortable question after uncomfortable question. The king of which was:

"Oh first date? Honey, are you on birth control?"

This was our first date

Eventually, the trio leaves and we giggle. We share a kiss that is interrupted with what I call, "Tequila's Revenge." It's not like she had a lot to drink, but the excitement of her wreck exasperated the situation.

"Can you take me home?" She asked.

"Sure."

On the drive back, she fought the urge to vomit. I prayed she doesn't ralph in my car. That would be the worst. Puke stink never leaves a car, and the alternative is insurance fraud for a new ride. Like a troop, she valorously battled her stomach.

Girl: 6 Failure: 0

As we turn into her apartment complex, she opened the door and expeled. None of it on my car.

Girl: 7 Failure: 0

I departed after making sure she got to her apartment. I text her the next day and thanked her for the amusing experience. She was mortified with the date. I take the opposite stance. She had a day where she could not suit up and act which, in turn, prevented me from doing the same. I appreciated the honesty of the experience.

Girl: 8 Failure: 0

The Secret to Fast and Permanent Weight Loss

Fox has somehow managed to lower the bar of programming to a level no one thought imaginable before. They have aired another reality show, entitled "More to Love." Allow me to explain the premise of the show. A dozen obese women compete for the affections of a younger version of John Goodman. The title of the show implies that heavier girls have something more to offer than an attractive female who knows when to put the Twinkie down.

This show parades these plus-sized females replete with all the mental issues unique to their appearance. The viewer is fed (yes, the pun was intended) boo-hoo stories of insecurities, loneliness, and desperation. Aside from triple digit dress sizes, they all lack one quality: DIGNITY. They cry about the fact they are alone, unwanted, and ugly. Yet the solution to their social ills lies in 4 simple words:

EAT LESS, MOVE MORE

My favorite is when they bemoan the fact they are ignored in the clubs. That is a lie. Men DO speak to them...as a vehicle to meet their thin and fine friends. If you are going to be on national TV, at least have the common decency to tell the truth in between trips to the buffet table.

What amazes me is when "More to Love" is aired...at dinner time! Last week's episode demonstrated the BBWs in swim suits. Hmmm...just what I want to see when I am eating! And right when you thought cottage cheese belonged on the plate and not someone's legs! It inspired me to throw my dinner away and just swallow a vitamin. Who sponsor's this crappy show? Ahh, during the commercial break, a Jenny Craig commercial came on! It mocks the premise of the show by leaving the viewer with this message:

"If you want to have a better chance of true love than these pathetic blobs, diet! Now! At least then you won't be gambling your future on the whims of a sleazy exploitative producer."

Fucking Brilliant!

I know not everybody can be a size 2. However, some of those women look so large; one wonders if they were performing an experiment of sorts. It's like as they grew in size, they deliberately enlarged other parts of their bodies; like the Incredible Hulk--minus the radiation and the muscles. Perhaps their train of thought went as follows:

"Wow! I am pretty fucking fat! I wonder if I can eat more, I can grow an extra body part. It's like cloning through calories. "

For the ladies who don't find love with 26 year old Fred Flintstone on "More to Love," I have a suggestion. It doesn't involve aerobics or an Oprah Winfrey juice yo- yo diet. If you want to find true love, get a World of Warcraft Account. There you will find available men with gallons of unspent sperm cells.

I know this as I am one of two skinny dudes who actually play!

PS. I know many of you who read this are thinking, "Jeeze Frank, you are a mean ASSHOLE!"
...to which I must reply, shallow too!

Adventures in Dating: The Creep Collection

I guess I was a squirrel in my past life as I have carried over the nut collecting skill into this one. Just recently, I had a scorned female wish me dead, and it inspired me to document all the mental cases that have gravitated to me over the years.

I. The Slave. As an undergraduate, I tried my hand at slave trading. I had attracted this female who would do anything for me. So, I had her cook dinner, drive me to school and wait while I attended classes. After school, she chauffeured me to and from work. While I enjoyed the power of human servitude, it did clash with what I learned in history: slavery was made illegal by the 13th Amendment.

So, I emancipated her.

I never imagined Abraham Lincoln having as much trouble as I did when I set just one slave free, and he freed an entire people! The slave didn't take her emancipation with the jubilee wrought by others of her condition. So, she stalked me. She arrived at my apartment, met me outside of class, and even tracked me down at work.

II. Creep Show. I met this girl in a bar a couple of years back, a hot little blonde bird, and all went swimmingly well until she offered to show me a picture of her son.

"Sure," I said.

Dutifully she reached into her bag and showed off the ugliest baby I had ever seen in my fucking life. That little bastard looked like Chuckie! It had toe nails for teeth, unkempt puppet hair, and a murderous sneer. "Jesus," I thought, "If something that ugly came out of your vagina, it must be broken."

The cherry on this shit pie was her son's name….

Elvis.

Yes, you read that right. The bitch named her Chuckie-ass looking kid Elvis. Her logic was this: her son was named after royalty.

I

Kid

You

Not

III. The Adventures of Tom Sawyer and Huckleberry Zoloft. I met an English teacher. Hey, you can't go wrong with that, right? Oh, I got an education in mental disability. I guess the first red flag was on our second date. We were just kissing, and she asked if I had protection.

"Nope," I replied. "I think we might want to stop here, I don't need any babies."

And with that last statement, her eyes froze, and her face contorted all Linda Blair-like. In demonic voice, she retorted, "What?! You don't want to have a kid with me?!!!"

This was only our second date, mind you.

Being a moron, I agreed to pick her up later that week for a third date. When I got to her apartment, she beckoned me to her computer to show off her wall paper.

It was a picture of my youngest daughter and me that she had copied from my Facebook profile. Right then I thought "you'll never meet my daughters….EVER!"

Needless to say, I thought it better to leave her alone with the voices in her head for company. My silence was paid back in threatening text messages, incessant calls, and "drive bys" in my apartment complex. It was kind of like living in a zombie movie where the undead hide just around the corner to take a menacing bite.

IV. Desperate Housewives of Stone Oak. With this one, I learned a couple of things. First, crazy people can live affluent areas. And second, booze and poor lighting does wonders for appearances. Skipping how I first encountered this gem, suffice to say that I met her for drinks. Once. In our discourse, she revealed that she was 12 years older than me. This fact led her to the revelation her privates don't work. Rust or some shit, I wasn't paying attention.

I felt just like Michael Scott in that Office Episode "Birthday Lunch." Look, I may be immoral swine, but I am no grave robber. I finished my beer and was content to let this one go back to the retirement home where senility would rob her of any memory of the night.

Then I received messages from beyond the grave….*plays supernatural-sounding music*

Every text, testified to her insecurities of being a solitary antique with a lonely death looming just around the corner. When I failed to respond to her cries for companionship, her texts turned threatening and hateful. I will display them for you:

Her: "I hope you get run over by a horseless carriage."

Me: "That is not very nice."

Her: "My first career was hexing pyramids to discourage thieves. Now I curse you with the Eye of Ra!"

Me: "I am sorry you feel that way"

Her: "Don't tell me what you think, whipper-snapper. Now get off of my lawn!"

So I am done. I am convinced all the good females are taken, leaving me with the remnant hordes of Charles Manson disciples. Forget it. If I ever feel the need to date, I'll log into the World of Warcraft and pay a Night Elf to dance for me.

A Traveler's Guide to there's United States
Part I

As I reflect on my travels, I have come to notice how each state in our beloved Union is as unique as the quarters patterned after them. As your friendly "Life-Reporter," I am obligated to point these idiosyncrasies out for your amusement and education.

Oklahoma

I believe we invaded the wrong piece of real estate in 2003. For national security purposes, the United States should have focused the full might and fury of its armed forces on the people of Oklahoma. To begin with, "Oklahoma" is an Indian word that means "Backwards." It is a state of contrasts. For instance, demonstrations of wealth are measured by how much random trash is strewn in the front lawn of your tin shack. The more rusty and dated the paraphernalia, the better. Middle class residents of Oklahoma only sport one junked car dating back to the Opec oil embargo of '73. The more affluent Oklahomans possess trucks from the Eisenhower Administration.

Oklahoma is the buckle of the Bible-belt states. It is so holy, they limit the alcohol content of their beer to 3%. When visiting Oklahoma, normal people can drink the amounts of beer a teenager typically lies about. I guess the good people in charge of Oklahoma believe that 3% beer solves all Satanic temptation. Yet, in a queer twist of logic, meth consumption is at an epic high. I'm not sure about that one.

Oklahoma is renowned for its Native American populations. Spotting the landscape, one can visit any number of Indian Reservations. In reality, no one goes for the culture of a dying people. They go to buy cheap smokes and post-cards.

I have polled people of Oklahoma and have found they excel at two hobbies: hunting and being kidnapped by Extra-Terrestrials. The irony does not escape me. A superior being hunts random mammals for sport while themselves being hunted by superior beings from another planet. I suppose it is the cycle of life.

Florida

When one thinks Florida, images of aged Jews and Cuban drug lords come to mind. That is media-induced stereotyping. In reality, when one visits Florida, one is inundated with aged Jews, Cuban drug lords, and shark attacks. Shark attacks in Florida are as common as meth junkies in Oklahoma. It makes me wonder about the tastes of these sharks and the wisdom of the aged Jews that are consumed. If I were a shark, I would prefer the taste of a fat little kid; not much gristle and the meat is still soft. It's kind of like veal. I don't think I would enjoy a dinner of leathery Jew flesh. It would taste gamey and be hard to chew.

As for the aged Jews inhabiting Florida, I miss the logic of their chosen place to die. These are a people who have a history of persecution spanning roughly 5,000 years. I can understand why they would not want to retire in Israel as the car bombs are plenty. But why choose such a dangerous local to await death? I'm sure there are safer places, like

Montana which only has 35 people. I find their logic in retirement communities to be masochistic. Shit! To me it would be as silly to retire in the ravenous waters of Florida as it would to purchase a summer home just outside of Auschwitz.

As for the Cuban drug lords, I have to thank Tony Montana as he gave me the greatest bed room line of all time. Just as I am pulling my dick out, I always quote him; "Say hello to my little friend!"

New Mexico

The problem with New Mexico is New Mexico. Stolen fair and square from Old Mexico, Mexicans laugh at what we inherited. To this day, if you read their newspapers you can find reference to it:

"Pinche gringos! Pueden tener Mexico Nuevo! Hay nada ahi pero criminales, y culebras!"

No one actually visits New Mexico, they drive through it on their way to more civilized locations. Years ago, in an effort to boost tourism, New Mexicans claimed to possess an alien crash site just outside of Roswell. We all know that is false as aliens do their partying in Oklahoma. So, in recent years, New Mexico has grown accustomed to their status as "on their way to somewhere else" state. Dotting the interstate are signs warning travelers not to pick up hitch hikers as they may be escaped prisoners. This leads one to wonder about the security of New Mexican prisons. If escapes are so common that they post signs warning people not to pick up convicts, do they teach how to escape in prison?

A Traveler's Guide to these United States
Part II

A continuation of my observations regarding the place we call home...

North and South Carolina

It is very important that we correctly distinguish the difference between North and South Carolina as we might stir the ire of rednecks on either side of the border. In North Carolina, the Hatfields only inbreed to the first cousin to keep the state's population of flipper-babies at an acceptable level. In South Carolina, the McCoys figure what the hell. Flipper babies happen!

The People's Democratic Republic of California

Have you ever noticed how the most repressive of Communist countries always include the phrase "People's Democratic Republic of?" It has nothing to do with the people nor the concept of a Republic. In Republics, people vote until someone like Julius Caesar comes along to fuck it all up.

California, like its brotherly states North Korea and Cuba, is home to all sorts of Big Brother protection laws. In the People's Democratic Republic of California it is against the law to smoke in bars. If you were to visit a club, you'd immediately notice that all of the patrons are on the back patio, leaving the three non-smokers inside enjoying the protection of California law.

Smart people buy their cars outside of the People's Democratic Republic of California and have them shipped in. This is because the emissions laws are so stringent that only the most weenie of engines can pass. Perhaps that is why has-beens like Ed Bagley drive those electric vaginas. All residents of the People's Democratic Republic of California live in constant fear of the dreaded "Tail-Pipe Gestapo" who live to fine wayward drivers. It makes me wonder how the hippies that infest San Francisco can drive their stupid '68 vintage Volkswagen Beatles to the Sanders rally without warming the Earth.

Alaska

Seward's Folly is a chunk of ice on top of a massive oil field. Yet, the Environmentalist hippies of the lunatic Left like paying $4 a gallon in gas. They claim that drilling for oil in Alaska would hurt the rich eco-system of an inhospitable chunk of ice where the temperatures might warm up to a cozy ten degrees. The only animal to have successfully managed to live in Alaska is that alien from John Carpenter's movie, "The Thing."

The tragedy of Alaska is akin to a dehydrated man in the desert and within reach of a pool of fresh water, only to have someone prohibit quenching his thirst. Remember the salad days of dollar a gallon gas? We could have that again! It is within our reach. I suggest the next time Nancy Pelosi complains about a national energy plan based on recycling our sandals, someone should grab her by the throat and scream, "Bitch! Let us drill! I'm sick of deciding whether or not is too expensive to drive to the grocery store! Fuck saving the alien from that John Carpenter movie, 'The Thing!' We need oil!"

On Star Trek

If I couldn't prove my nerd credentials anymore; I've actually taken some time to analyze the Star Trek Universe. Yes, I have squandered a university-trained mind to ponder stupid shit. Here are some of my findings:

1. Why would the skipper of a ship beam down into a hostile situation? Isn't he needed to command the crew under his command? Moreover, why does he continually feel the need to take all the senior officers with him? Who is left in command while the officers are gallivanting on the planet? Perhaps the 17-year old fresh-out-of basic junior sailor?

2. All service branches have intelligence officers to gather information for command decisions. Star Fleet lacks this. Instead they rely "brain storming sessions." Kirk then decides his crew's fate based on a hunch.

3. Star Trek aliens are the weakest EVER! They have a race called Romulans from planet Romulus. Hmm, what a coincidence. In our history we had Romans whose mythical founder was Romulus. In the original show, they had Klingons that looked more like Mexican stereotypes with ray guns. However, in the movies, Klingons still look like Mexican bandits, but with tiny spines on their heads.

4. Captain Kirk is a man worth my admiration. He drinks, fuck, and beats the shit out of people. His behavior is the foundation of my moral outlook. Captain Pickard, however, could NEVER live up to be the man Kirk embodies. Pickard

spends his time reading boring classical literature at the expense of getting his dick wet. He would rather negotiate problems rather than solve them as a MAN would. As a matter of fact, Pickard is the dullest person in the Universe. I do believe the Federation of Planets stayed safe from alien invasion because it harbored the most boring person in the galaxy. Here is how this plays out:

Alien Invader: "Enterprise, you have no choice. We are going to invade Earth and enslave its population."

Captain Pickard: "In all of our history, we have found an alternative to violence. Allow me to quote Shakespeare to make my point...."

Alien Invader: "ZZzzzzzzzz...."

5. With a crew compliment of over 500 hands, why is it that the only people who do any work on the Enterprise the same five people on the bridge? The rest do absolutely NOTHING! That sounds a lot like the Space Force. Where can I join?

6. Where does Star Fleet find the morons to fill the "guys in red shirts who always get killed ranks?" I guess from the same pool of idiots that aspire to be ISIS. This also begs the question, how does Star Fleet recruit for the "red is dead" cannon fodder?

Star Fleet Recruitment Poster
--Join up and see the galaxy! We can promise you regular pay, college tuition, and a short career!

7. Why does the ship surgeon always loiter on the

bridge? Shouldn't he be in sick bay taking care of...the sick!
Even under attack, McCoy can be found on the bridge
offering fake rural wisdom for any given situation.
Meanwhile, legions of lazy ass crewmen perish of their
wounds.

First Love

I am going to make a huge departure from the style of my usual musings and try something different. A good author will seek challenges, and since I fancy myself a bit of a wordsmith, I gladly accept.

Most of my readers know me to be the one who put the Ass in Asshole. To them, I offer this: cynics are not born, they are made. A true Curmudgeon is born to the parents of personal tragedy and the failures of those they love. It's a sad combination whose offspring have come to expect being shortchanged by others.

Thus I am led to the point of this discourse. Do any of you remember your very first love? You know, the one that really stuck. The one whose name you will never forget. The one who you still wonder about from time to time?
I do.

Her name was Anna. I can still remember her phone number, even though it has been well over twenty years since I used it. There is something about that very first one that never lets you forget. Years can pass; relationships begin and end; life clouds your memories; but somehow that one lurks beneath it all. It's not like you spend every moment pining for them. It's more like they are restless spirits who haunt your thoughts, and no matter how much you try to bury them, they remain unchanged by time or experience. I am a hard man with little sympathy for others nor empathy to spare. Yet even I find myself a victim of this haunting from time to time.

Frank Swanson

I loved that woman. As a matter of fact, it is fair to say that I loved her more than my wife and the mother of my children. I think Cindy knew this, although we never spoke about it. I loved everything about her; perfect porcelain skin, deep brown eyes, jet black hair, and her laugh. In fact, I can remember how she smelled if I think hard enough. Winter green. She smelled like fresh winter green. After we parted company she forgot a sweater at my apartment. At times, I would push my face into it, robbing it of her scent.

Memories can be comforting and cruel at the same time. They flash by in a disjointed movie. Every time I would drop her off after a date, I'd gloomily say good bye and she would remind me, "For every good bye, there is a hello." One day, there were no more hellos.

Our first time was scary, wondrous, innocent, and yet felt just right. The honesty of the experience is what I remember most.

She held me in the rain when my mom kicked me out of the house. College scared me in my first semester; I didn't think I was up to the task. Anna's encouragement helped me overcome that fear and earn straight A's that first semester. I'd wake up to her snuggling next to me. The break up proved to be a first lesson in loss. It hurt physically, like being swarmed by thousands of angry bees and feeling lost at the same time. But, like with all things; as time passed, the experience dulled.

Years passed. I grew in relationships, joined the military, married and never thought in my wildest dreams I would ever encounter Anna again.

I was wrong.

In a shoe store with my wife and youngest daughter I heard her voice. Even though I hadn't talked to her in over two decades, and I was distracted by other things, I recognized that voice. It felt like getting kicked in the stomach. It was not painful, mind you; more of a blow that felt familiar and distant at the same time. I froze. I looked at my wife and pointed to the woman walking by.

"That was Anna."

Cindy cast a disapproving glare at her. Even though age had made its mark on Anna I do believe my wife fought a brief bout of jealousy. I don't blame her. "Well, at least you have a cute and skinny wife." Cindy said with confidence.

What did I do?

Nothing.

I was scared. What would Anna say to me? Would she disapprove or dismiss me? After twenty years, what do you say to someone who was once so intimate?

I chose the coward's way out.

I collected my daughter and left. I didn't tell my wife about this, but I secretly returned to that location, hoping I could find her and tell her that after all these years, she still impacted me. I wasn't sure what I would say or how I would say it; all I knew was that I wanted Anna to know that I existed and she meant so much to me.

I never found her.

Frank Swanson

Border Security

I loathe illegal aliens. They swarm into our country with a cultural commitment to crime like it's their constitutional right to rape, pillage, and plunder. Our national policy over it is a complete joke. If you think I am referring to our friends south of the Rio Grande, you are wrong. I am talking about ALIEN aliens. You might know them as E.T.s or Extra-Terristicles. They are the real threat.

Presidential Candidate Donald Trump promised to build a wall on the US-Mexican border. Left unchecked are hundreds if, not thousands, of little grey bubble-headed space aliens that do far worse than harvest cotton. Those fuckers break into people's houses. They sexually violate their victims, and leave the scene before the police arrive. Donald Trump misses the point. I don't see Juan Gomez standing in my room armed with a metal rod to shove up my ass. Instead, he can be found on the street peddling fresh fruit. I like fresh fruit; it is good, and good for you.

Space alien abductions are the REAL threat to border security. Every day they come to the US in search of fun and excitement like the Earth is some sort of intergalactic Spring Break destination where any Caligula-esque sin is indulged. If we could speak Alien an abduction works as follows:

Alien 1: "We have this human female strapped to the table. What can we do that we haven't already done? I am getting bored."

Alien 2: "I think I have my jump drive from my physics class in my room. Wanna stick that up her ass?"

I wonder, do they take snapshots of their shenanigans and post them on some sort of Alien network like Facebook,

Mars edition?

"My name is Bleark and my hobbies are cruising around in my '73 Saucer, romantic comedies, and sticking shit up the rectums of human prey. I like traveling until my old ride broke down in Roswell."

If you ask me, I say forget the illegal Mexicans. The most you can get from them is a tummy ache from spoiled fruit. Let's focus on aliens because being butt raped by some owl-eyed pervert is a lot more menacing.

Frank Swanson

Grocery Store Observations

The grocery store can be a boundless source of amusement if you pay attention. In fact, if you are in the right mind, a trip to buy groceries can be an outright adventure. When one passes the Deli section, there is an island manned by Asians who cut and package sushi. At times they offer free samples, yet jealously guard their pride of Asia, from sampler hogs. I sometimes wonder why only Asians work the sushi stand. Sushi is a food and all foods can be replicated by anyone despite ethnicity. It's as if HEB food cooperation is telling their customers:

"We have captured specially trained Asians in the wilds of the Himalayas to provide our customers the most authentic sushi outside of Asia."

Rather racist to say the least.

As I continued my voyage around the enslaved Asian sushi makers, I picked up a coupon. HEB marries the most random shit together in order to move products. For instance, one coupon might read:

"With the purchase of 9 rolls of Hill Country Toilet Paper, get 1 three ounce cup of Sour Cream."

Yeah, when I am wiping my ass, sour cream ALWAYS comes to mind.

Checking out is no easy task either. I witnessed the ultimate fail of American education as it cut in front of me in the 10 items or less line. Stuffed in his basket were 30 items. I resisted the violent urge to throttle him by his corpulent neck and scream: "You fat mother fucker! This is the 10 items or less line! So which is it? You either can't count or can't fucking read!"

As I wait for the illiterate and math challenged customer to be processed, I notice magazine headlines with asinine headlines like:

"Eat food and lose weight!" What the fuck?

Finally I reach the checkout lady. On cue she tempts me to purchase a disposable camera. A disposable camera was a hot seller back in 1976. Really, how old is their marketing czar? I am surprised if the next time I check out at HEB the cashier doesn't offer me a deal on parchment and quills. When confronted with the hot disposable camera, I said, "No thank you ma'am. I am from the future, and I have traveled here to offer you barbaric savages the miracle of digital cameras."

Frank Swanson

Netflix

Cheap entertainment is hard to come by these days. In these challenging economic times, the only people who can afford vacations anymore are CEOs, doctors and high school football coaches. With entertainment coming at a premium, middle and lower class people have to scrounge for cheap alternatives. After all, not all of us can draw Xs and Os for a living and make $70,000 a year. On an average night, many Americans look to Netflix as an escape from the hum drum of everyday life. But, with the recent price hike of Netflix streaming videos, have any of you people taken notice of the crap they are offering?

In essence, I pay $20 a month for Netflix to shit on me. I don't need to see the controversial internet video, "Two Girls, One Cup." With my Netflix membership, I fucking live it!

On the surface, Netflix streaming videos offer a lot of options. It's kind of like being condemned to death and having the ability to choose your execution. The guillotine might be faster, but hemlock poisoning is relatively painless. Welcome to your Netflix streaming account! The movies are so bad that actual suicide is a plausible alternative. Yes, I would rather hang myself than suffer through some of the crap the Netflix Board of Directors deem "entertainment."

Every month, I am snookered into their "New Arrivals." You want to know what Netflix considers new arrivals? Here is a partial list with the year these movies were made:
King Kong (1976)
The Wolf man (1941)

Dracula (1933)

Son of Frankenstein (1939)

If those movies are new, then I am a 40 year old toddler. Who is their marketing director, some time traveling cheapskate from the 70s that raids the bargain bin DVD selections at the local grocery store? You know what I am talking about; it's the graveyard where the careers of Chuck Norris and Branden Frazier have come to rest. These movies are to new what Steve Jobs is to breathing.

Even a cursory glance at the other movies in the queue reveals how shameless Netflix can be in their selections. Some of these titles are so bad that even Bollywood—infamous for churning out thousands of tacky movies a year—wouldn't touch. Some of them are just blind rip offs of more successful movies that attempt to web a victim into believing it actually played in a theater somewhere. For instance, Children of the Corn was a movie made in the 80s that actually had an audience. You can't find that movie on Netflix, but you can see Children of the Corn 7. What the fuck? I didn't know there were 6 sequels. Did I miss something? Probably not. Children of the Corn episodes 2-6 probably earned dozens of dollars.

Sometimes, to capitalize on a real movie's success, Netflix sneaks in a cleverly titled sham to lasso those customers who think their $20 a month might buy some actual entertainment. For those who liked "Paranormal Activity" Netflix can underwhelm them with "Paranormal Entity." It's almost the same movie, just without the character development, coherent plot, suspense, or interest.

Other Netflix selections are just plain odd. Being an intelligent man, I like the occasional documentary. With the bland selections I am forced to choose from, I am convinced that I have more taste in my penis. Who wants to watch a biography of Conrad Hilton? He built hotels. And?! Who gives two fucks? I could choose the "Buena Vista Social Club," a documentary about Cuban musicians. Yawn, I've seen I Love Lucy as well, and have had my fill of the Cuban antics of Ricky Retardo. Another riveting Netflix title won numerous awards at the South by Southwest Music festival. Called Pelada, it traces the exciting adventures of soccer fans who travel the world meeting other soccer fans and finding out how much they have in common............................

...........zzzzz...........Opps. Sorry, I dozed for a moment.

The market for magical Asian movies has found its place in the Netflix cue. We are bombarded with Hong Kong actions stars like Jet Li, and Takayuki Yamada. Every Kung Fu movie imaginable is available here. All of these Netflix snoozers have one thing in common; if you learn karate, it enables one to defy Newtonian physics and biomechanics.

So what is the solution? In one word: Piracy. If Hollywood would produce something worth watching, I'd be less inclined to steal it on the internet. Netflix offers the worst in entertainment. They are why internet pirates exist.

Just Spit Balling Here

Adventures in Dating: The POW Experience

First, I must admonish myself of something I swore off of long ago:

"I will not meet girls in bars."
"I will not meet girls in bars."
"I will not meet girls in bars."
I will write that 100 more times until it is programmed into my brain as naturally as breathing.

So I met this girl at a bar. We held a brief conversation about music and tattoos before we set up a date later in the week. That's all I remember about that part, as well...you know how that goes.

Denise arrived at La Hacienda sporting a blouse that revealed every tattoo she had. I can't complain, as I am pretty tatted up myself. However, there are places where women shouldn't get tattoos:

1. The boob area. That screams trailer and leads one to wonder how many times you have appeared on the Springer Show

2. The upper arm. That communicates, "I drive a semi truck for a living, and meth gets me through the long hauls."

Yes, she violated both of those social mores.

The conversation started awkward and only got worse from there. Over the course of lunch and a couple of beers, she pipes up and declares: "I can tell you are like a manly kind of guy. I like that, because if you weren't I'd walk all over ya."

Having been married for 7 years, I do speak a little girl. When a female says, "I'll walk all over you, she really means

'I AM A STARK RAVING BITCH.'"

She then describes why her last relationship went sour. "I am a total fag hag and my best friend is a gay guy addicted to meth. My last boyfriend slept with him and..."

Me: *There ya go! Take that whole bucket of crazy sauce and dump it in all in my lap. Don't miss a drop. Don't miss a f**king drop!*

I tried to steer the conversation back to some sense of normality. "So you like the Misfits. I am a huge fan, only when Glenn Danzig sung for them."

Denise countered, "I liked them better with Neil Armstrong."

?????????????????

"I think you're confusing the guy who landed on the moon--"

"--No, I am sure of it." She declared.

Okay, Neil Armstrong landed on the moon and hung up a career in science to sing for a punk rock band. We'll go with that.

I've already decided this will go nowhere, but since she was obviously nuttier than squirrel shit, it would be amusing to push it further in the interest of mocking her later. I voluntarily submitted myself as a Prisoner of War, and let her drive me to her home. You assholes better appreciate this!

We end up at her place--an apartment complex decorated with trash on the grounds and Vietnamese boat people milling about. We walk inside and decided to watch a movie. This is where she challenged my man card.

"I'll let you hook up the DVD player. That is man work and I refuse to do it."

A note to all females. Just because our plumbing is an "outie" does not make us your TV repairman, wood worker, lawn care expert, or car mechanic. I went to college, and I pay mother fuckers who didn't, to perform those tasks. Since matching the red wire to the red hole befuddled her, I hooked up the TV and we watch a movie about some psycho little girl who cuts up people and makes dolls out of their body parts.

How fitting

In the middle of the movie, there is a knock at the door. Denise answered it, and in walk Nikki Sixx and Eminem. Ok, they weren't REALLY Nikki Sixx and Eminem, just two douche bag twenty-somethings who dressed like Nikki Sixx and Eminem. They introduced themselves and gave me their names, but I forgot them. I figure if you want to look like Nikki Sixx and Eminem, I'll just remember you as Nikki Sixx and Eminem.

Denise, Nikki Sixx, and Eminem all chat about what they plan to do for the evening. Nikki Sixx and Eminem were headed out to Club Rotting Corpse or some shit like that. When they left, Denise confided: "I slept with Nikki Sixx for a while, but not anymore."

Me : *Of course you did.*

We settle down and finish the movie. She props up her feet on the table and I notice she hasn't cleaned her toenails since the Clinton Administration. "Yeah," I think, "If you could just run a file under those toes that would be greaat!

It's now bedtime, and I've already decided I wouldn't touch her with my worst enemy's penis. Remember, he ex boyfriend had sex with a needle-using guy, and she also had sex with Nikki Sixx. That is a recipe for an alphabet soup of diseases: VD, HIV, AIDS, etc. There are degrees of protection for sexual contact:

1. Condom
2. Plastic Bubble
3. Military MOPP suit
4. Space Suit--the kind Neil Armstrong used when he sung for the
f**king Misfits

Denise rated at least 2 Number 4's. It didn't matter in any event as she went to the bathroom and returned with the announcement, "I just started my period."--Thus ending any residual worth she held as a human being.

Now get this. She offered to let me sleep in her bed. I go to her room and instantly fear for my life. On the wall is a poster of a guy with a knife. "Oh great," I wonder. "I bet she's stabby." My Discovery ID survival mode kicks into gear.

...and it only gets better.

"If you need to use the bathroom, the red stuff splashed all over the walls is not blood, it's hair dye."

She said this.

I

Shit

You

Not.

As we settle in, she entertains me by reading texts from her drug addicted gay friend:

"I'm ok when I use...."

Me: *Shut up*

Denise reads on: "It's not like I ice all the time, just a bump or two a day—"

Me: *For the love of God, shut the fuck up.*
Denise read more: "I'll get clean of this in my own time--
"

Me: *If you don't shut up, I'll snatch the life right out of you*
Denise put the phone down and offered me some street-purchased xanax to help me sleep.

"No," I reply, "I do not want illegal prescription drugs, but thanks anyway."
Finally sleep, and even that was f**ked up. This bitch didn't just snore--she snarled. I'm talking Little Nicky snarling that scared the shit out of me. I tried to record it, but every time I attempted to she'd quiet down.
As you can see, I did make it out alive. And I think I'm going to quit teaching and enter a monastery. I am done with crazy people

Frank Swanson

Adventures in Dating: The POW
Experience....Liberation Day

This is a continuation of my last horrendous date. There was so much awful packed into one night that two blogs are required to tell the tale. Besides, you know how narratives of traumatic events are built over time with intense therapy sessions until the whole story can be fleshed out? You know the kind:

Uncle Mike touched me there, and there....

Aliens visited me at night and probed me...

That was how I felt spending the night with Denise. I was traumatized, and I'll be visiting the VA for a diagnosis of PTSD.

After lunch, she offered to drive me to her house. However, before we did that, I needed to pick up a few things at my apartment. I invited her in. As I packed an overnight bag, she wandered around. She pointed at my wall and asked, "Are these your pussy magnets?"

????????????

"No," I reply. "What you are pointing at is a Bachelor's of Art Diploma, an Honorable Discharge Certificate, and a couple of commendation awards."

You see, I can understand her awe at real accomplishments. She was, after all, a student of massage therapy where the final exam concluded with "happy endings." I hop in her giant boat-car, and off we go. I am not kidding, the bitch drove a f**king 1970s era yacht. It was so old the radio didn't play anything newer than ABBA.

After we watch creepy movies and are visited by Nikki

Sixx and Eminem it's about 11:00. At that point I had a realization; which under any other circumstance would be horrible.

I was poop pregnant.

The onset of male pregnancy is not a union of sperm and egg. Rather, it is a blending of Mexican food and beer which combined to form a monster welling up in my belly.

Now mind you, if she was fine I could manage my gastro-intestinal tract like a Zen Master. However, since this woman was swine, I felt no moral obligation to withhold my bodily flavors. So I go to the bathroom and give man birth to my tar child. I put that toilet to shame, and the noxious vapors that filled the apartment were so toxic that if I were to bottle them up, I am reasonably sure I could be convicted of a war crime. Not only that, this one was a dirty bastard. It was one of those craps where wipe number 37 came out just as filthy as wipe number one. I literally flushed the toilet 8 times and went through an entire roll of toilet paper. I didn't even finish cleaning up. I was spending the night with Denise, after all.

Being the crass pig she was, Denise commented on how foul the bathroom smelled.

I feigned sorrow, but in reality I hoped I was the nastiest mother f**ker to have ever disgraced her toilet.

I awake the next morning, and I am just glad I was:

1. Not stabbed

2. Not violated by Nikki Sixx or Eminem.

So my next plan was to get out of there--quickly! I mumble something about having to pick up the kids by 10.

As Denise dressed, she asked: "What time do you have to get your kids?"

Me: "9:30."

Just get me out of here, please Dear God!

Just as we leave her apartment, I notice crude drawings on the wall right outside of her door. They were chalk-drawn penises, the kind you see on art assignments at the end of a school year. I wondered why someone would take the time to draw them. Are they like Hobo signs communicating to other Hobos? It's like a communication to other miscreants that says, "You can use this here."

On the drive home, Denise attempts to make conversation. "My gay needle meth friend just texted me and said he misses me like a fat boy misses cake."

Me: Blank stare

"I had a blast last night. We'll have to do it again!"

Me: *You Pig! I took the nastiest shit ever in your apartment and you want to see ME again?*

We pass Sugars. It's a stripper bar. Denise announces, "I love that place!"

Me: *Of course you do.*

Denise: "Well, I could never strip myself, but I have nothing against strippers per say."

Me: *Wait. You literally told me you slept with like 532 men, half of which are on drugs. Public nudity is where you draw the line?*

Denise: "I did strip one night of course, but I was all coked up."

Me: *Keep it classy*

People I Hate, Volume I

Methanie Skelefield

One of the benefits to divorce is not only can you cut out your spouse's fucked up family out of your life quicker than a malignant cancer, but their equally dysfunctional friends as well. Just the other day, this creature sent me an email and a friend request on Facebook. In her disjointed, methamphetamine-fueled message, she attempted to assuage her past injustices by saying it was, "water under the bridge."

Yeah, if that water was a river of blood and this were the end of fucking times.

That's exactly what this bitch is, a creature ripped straight from Revelations. Methanie Skelefield is that 5th Horseman of the Apocalypse that St. John was too terrified to mention:

"Lo, there was a 5th Horseman that Lucifer begat onto the world. It rode a rusty trailer onto the fields of Armageddon. It spewed crystals from its eyes that caused a great speeding amongst the sinners. Worms grew from their skin, and thus they scratched."

Prior to her costarring with War and Famine, I first encountered Methanie on a double date with her husband, the Hannah Barbarra cartoon, Grape Ape. My first impression of her proved spot on—a soulless Ginger. Her teeth looked like jagged toe nails, and her eyes were so wide apart I wondered what supporting role she played on Finding Nemo. Her body looked like it was built by a retarded understudy of Dr. Frankenstein: giant man-arms, deformed bubble butt, and a chest that could rival the mummified remains of King Tut. The most ironic aspect of Methanie was how she made her money—stripping.

At the time she danced at a place called Camelot, located just outside the front gate of Randolph Air Force Base. That made sense. Most strip bars adjacent to any military post usually host carnival freaks. Savvy businessmen know GI's aren't that discerning, so that allows for these abominations. They can have 3 titties, be pregnant with a litter, or sport two fucking heads. It doesn't matter, the money keeps rolling in.

If this weren't enough, this 5th Horseman of the Apocalypse had a kid. Her and Grape Ape produced a saber-toothed primate that was a couple of evolutionary steps down from Homo Sapiens. Like her mother, this vile breeding of demon and cartoon had a temper that served as a personality. I can't blame the kid for its temperament; in the argument between nature vs. nurture, she was a double-loser.

We all know how awful people can be in the middle of a divorce. Yet this avenging Horseman of the End of Times was present to defend my ex wife.

One day, I was pulled out of class by my principal. Apparently, there was a parent irate about my performance, and she demanded a conference call. That angry parent turned out to be Methanie Skelefield. No, her child was not a student of mine. In fact, I doubt she'd graduated from potty training much less into the low standards set by the public school system. Methanie was on the tail end of a tweaker as I listened in on the conference call.

Methanie: "Frank is on MySpace and he has pictures of himself with guns! Do you think it's good to have your teachers showing off guns?"

My Principal looks at me and I say, "Yeah, guilty as charged. I do have a picture of me when I was at Camp Pendleton. I had a service rifle slung over my shoulder. It's part of the job."

Enraged with this response, Methanie then issued the most ridiculous threat ever: "I'll come up there with my posse and embarrass him!"

My principal assured Methanie that her and her posse would be removed by the police, thus foiling any plans she had for humiliation. I giggled and wondered what posse? Perhaps she meant the narcotic-born worms that kept her company as she scratched. No one besides Grape Ape could even stand the bitch.

Years later she sent me a friend request on Facebook. I don't know why. Perhaps she felt the dust had settled concerning my divorce, and she felt entitled to rekindle her idea of friendship. Explaining that is like explaining schizophrenia. Perhaps I'll accept it—and let her read this blog.
Hilarity can only ensue.

The Sexy Apartment Manager Conundrum.

I had my eyes on a woman.   And this one is proving to challenge my shallowness in ways I never imagined before. She is my apartment manager. She is employed, pretty, warm, and friendly. So what could the problem be, you might ask.

The problem is, she is big. I don't mean big like her ass warrants congressional representation big. I mean big in that she eats regularly. She is deformed, but only slightly so. Yet the fact remains, she is deformed. It would be like dating a girl with 11 fingers. You can only ignore deformities for so long before they kill any potential romance.

This places me in a conundrum. Do I ignore her physical impairment and attempt to forge an inter-species relationship? When I ask her out, should I suggest an activity that might be therapeutic for her? "Hey, how about we spend a couple of hours on the treadmill?" I just don't know what to do. My fear is that if I accept her as she is, she might get comfortable and expand like a water-logged nerf ball.

Whenever I am in need of relationship advice, I contact my friend Jen. Not only does she know me, she has two masters degrees, and is currently a doctoral candidate. Surely that wealth of learned knowledge can offer some guidance in my current crisis. When I explain my situation, she offered the following analysis:

"You're a dick."

She went on to say I should accept her the way she is, appreciate her as a person, and a bunch of other Oxygen Network crap that I ignored. Guys who think like that already have boyfriends.

So I made a pro versus con list concerning the apartment manager. Here it is:

Pros:

1. She is pretty if I only look at her face and avoid the penis-wilting rest of her

2. I could possibly get her to commit fraud by counting my rent as paid. I could use that extra money to flirt with other girls.

Cons:

1. She is deformed.

The point was almost moot a couple of months ago when I decided to ask her out to a place where no one I know would ever be found. However, every time I ventured into the office to pay rent, or complain about my toilet, her co-manager always intercepted me. Let me describe her. The Co-manager is a big monster that should be featured on the Discovery Channel. Her belly button could serve as a bean dip bowl with a week's worth of left-overs. Whenever I went into the office, she'd scurry out to talk to me faster than Jabba finds Han Solo. She operated like an obese ninja in her cock-blocking swiftness. "Jesus," I thought, "You think I just bathed in bacon."

Perhaps the co-manager is my guardian angel whose corpulent interventions are keeping me on the straight and narrow. Perhaps it's God's way of saying, "Don't do it! Don't do it, ya bastard!"

I don't know what to do. Do I ask her out for low-carb dates in the hope the Apartment Manager avoids diabetes and I can slim her down? Do I forget it altogether in the interest of not being evicted?

I am so confused…

Barracks Tales, Part I: The Guardian

If any of you have ever been in the military, you are the first to know that uniformed service attracts some of the craziest people on the planet. I'm not sure why, nor am I inclined to figure it out. All I know is that I came across all the crazies. Seriously, all of them.

For those enlisting into the military, I have a bit of advice; make rank fast. Enlisted grades E-1 through E-4 are Uncle Sam's way of taking your youthful patriotic vigor, and giving you the finger. For example, the housing my recruiter lied to me about was fucking awful. Every junior troop is quartered in slums so terrible that I am reasonably sure they would be condemned in Kenya. I stayed in a dingy, two man dorm with one shower and toilet shared by the other 200 suckers on that floor.

I reported to my gaining command; a fresh new troop who was ready to save Western Civilization as we know it. When given the key to my quarters, I entered and found a huge black guy lying naked on his bed. No sheets, no towel, nothing to cover him up: He lay there indifferent to my appearance. He was motionless, engaged in the adventures of Ren and Stempy as it played on the TV. Most people— guided by social mores—might be urged to conceal his junk.

Not this guy. He laid there; nude and oblivious to my presence.

"Would you mind covering up, Dude?" I ask politely.

No response.

"Really, I am just here for a few days, and I don't want to spend my sleeping hours with your junk hanging out."

No response.

I considered the fact he might be dead—which for a government-run operation—might hold true. But his eyes did move as Ren and Stempy continued their adventures. Typical, I reason. This is me after all.

Every morning, I'd leave for work and come back. Awaiting me as I returned was this comatose black guy who just laid there. Naked. He didn't change positions. All the while I had to live with the uncomfortable and awkward feeling of his penis lumped over his thigh, facing me.

Have you ever passed by a portrait in a museum and get the creepy feeling that its eyes were following you? That is how I felt as time progressed. It was like that guy's member was watching me. Its one, squinty eye vigilantly tracking my every movement, almost daring me to change the channel or disturb its master. Its threatening glare prevented me from altering its environment. I was afraid it would attack me. Seriously, I imagined it might hop off its Host and come bite me. Maybe this guy was nothing more than a life support system for his member, like something you'd see in Men in Black.

Perhaps he was an alien.

I pulled the sheets over my head every night, hoping it would be enough to shield me from a bite. I think it worked. I emerged unscathed from the master and its guardian.

Alma Mater

So I attended my high school reunion and found the event lacking in assholes, psychos, or misfits. In fact, I found everyone there to be pleasant, articulate, and kind. It's quite a stretch for me to interact with anyone without some sort of mental or emotional issue, so the experience was novel.

For this to make any sense, I have to give a little back story.

I didn't consider high school to be that important. In fact, I breezed through my university education with the same kind of indifference I did in grades 9 through 12. My real education came on my own through life experiences. Like thousands of others, I was just getting my ticket stamped to ensure a middle class life. As an intelligent, albeit undisciplined child, I spent most of my time in high school either suspended, in the luxury jail known as "in school suspension," or in some other ineffective institutional behavioral correction program. My offenses had a central theme: not playing well with others.

I was bored and too lazy to enroll in challenging classes. I knew my financial means were slight, so why kill myself to get accepted into Harvard when my future belonged to a state university? It was a comfortable arrangement that allowed me to be creative in petty crime with the foreknowledge that ensured acceptance into a 4-year college. Win, win!

Who did I choose to surround myself with in those formative years?

Assholes.

My high school friends didn't attend the reunion, mostly because of parole conditions. They nursed decades-long heroin habits, which is why I parted company with them. I've always hated drugs. To me, they were symbolic of the hippie assholes who called Vietnam veterans "baby killers." My father just about crippled one stupid enough to pull that stunt. Note to hippies: if you feel the need to insult a service man, avoid the ones with green berets.

That being said, my reunion was populated with people who got it right. I knew almost none of them. I felt like Columbus, deciding which native he wanted to get lucky with first. Upon walking in, I find my old acquaintance, M, who I knew from middle school. She pretty much set the theme for the night. She had read my blogs over the years, and her character judgement proved apt.

M as she introduced me to another acquaintance: "This is Frank. He is a Douche Bag."

I love honesty from people. If it were more prevalent, the world would be a better place. As a matter of fact, I was introduced to a number of people with the title "Douche Bag." Okay, I have to own that one. I know what I am. Since I wore the crown proudly, I decided to live up to the role. Then I happened upon Beer Girl.

Beer Girl is a sweetheart, who just happened to be at the wrong place at the wrong time. I goaded her to kiss me years ago, and I thought this was easy prey. Surely she could feed on how pleased I am with myself.

Me: "When are we finally gonna hook up? You know I am the best looking mother f**ker here."

Beer Girl: "I'm not debating that, but we can't."

Me: "You have got to be kidding. Why?"

Beer Girl: "Your music scares me."

Me: "Just because I listen to Slayer doesn't mean I cum in lava."

Beer Girl: "We can't because you'll write about me."

Me: "Duh!"

I found myself a victim of modest rants on a social media website. That is a common complaint. In fact, this is why M introduced me as a Douche Bag. As I circled around various people at the reunion, many complimented me on my writing. One told me it was his favorite literature while clearing his bowels. That about nails it—my thoughts are held in the same regard as fecal discharge. I agree.

The other person of note was Blonde. I like Blonde. She is hot; has a chest that inspires infants to cry, and that animal attraction that motivates vampires. Not the gay ones found in Twilight, mind you. I am talking full-on Bela Legosi. There is only one problem with Blonde.

She is married.

Blonde is unlike many married women. She is loyal. I can appreciate that, and despite being a Douche, I do understand boundaries. Still, I have to stifle my normal impulses. If there is one thing I do not jack with, it's marriage.

Then I met another kindred spirit. She went from high school hooligan to an assistant principal. Holy shit, this transformation was almost too good to be believed. Our conversation was comedic:

Assistant Principal: "I heard you became a teacher." Her tone denoted something more along the lines of: "I heard you were a paraplegic, and set the world record mile."

Me: "Yeah, I am the sheriff of Six Flags too!"

So I left, but I had a plan in mind. I texted "Old Faithful" to come over. Old Faithful is someone who thinks she is a real human being, but she's not.

It's funny when women think that. The whole idea of certain women attempting to grow a self esteem is evident here.

She texted me back with this gem: "To you I am just a hole."

Me: "No you mean more than that. You are like 3 of them. Now come over."

Unburdened by thinking, she did!

It was a great reunion!

Dexter—The Verdict is…..GUILTY!

I just finished binge watching 8 seasons of Dexter. I thought the original idea, novel—an "everyman" serial killer. However, as the seasons wore on, and the writers ran out of source material, the show devolved into comedic drivel. While criticizing every iota of idiocy would require a book, here are some of the most egregious examples.

Racism

Yes, I said it. Dexter is a racist show. Its sloppy treatment of minority characters might make excellent viewing….

…if this was 1938…in Berlin.

First, I am not sure if the writers are familiar with Cuban culture. Take Officer Angel Batista for example. I am convinced Batista is a name they farmed from Wikipedia. Second, he is a walking cliché, exemplified by his stupid Fedora hat. When asked why he wore a Fedora, even in the shower, Officer Batista answered, "It's a reflection of my Cuban heritage."

What?

The only thing a Fedora reflects is wardrobe design from the set of 1963's "Goldfinger." He drinks to excess, and is prone to flare-ups of his hot "Latin temper." Why not just add some cocaine and have him say, "Mang" every other word, and your stereotype is complete.

Erik King could only do so much with his character, Officer Doakes. In essence, his role was to play, "angry black man." We are not given insight into why Officer

Doakes carries a huge black chip on his shoulder. We are just left to believe that his anger stems from…..being black?

Oh, and guess who is framed as a serial killer? You got it! Officer Doakes, because OJ.

I'm sure the nitwit writers will attempt to rectify some of these issues should a movie version of Dexter ever emerge. They would probably introduce such clumsy characters as:

Officer Ory Entall. Officer Ory Entall is not only the Department's math whiz, he heads the table tennis league as well.

Officer Meshuga $$$$-berg. Officer $$$$-berg is the Department's finance officer, and he'll keep the rates reasonable.

Dumbest Cops in the History of Police Work

If I ever decide to become a serial killer, I'll practice my craft in Miami. Guess how many murders they solved?

Zero.

Better police work can be found in a game of Clue than in all of the Miami Homicide Division: "It was Colonel Mustard in the Kitchen with a knife." These cops couldn't solve a murder without Dexter's help. They could roll up on the body of a decapitated murder victim. Five feet away, Jeffery Dahmer could be having sex with its head, and the detectives would scratch their chins, proclaiming: "My hunch tells me….."

Dexter's sister walked into a police station and confessed to the Capital Murder of a fellow police officer. Miami Homicide's reaction?

"She got jokes."

Dexter himself murdered a guy INSIDE the police station. I suppose Miami police pioneered killing suspects in custody before it became popular.

Bad Writing

After the writers ran out of source material, they got real strange with it. My question is which writer thought incest should be a theme? Not incest in the deplorable sense of the word, but sneaky incest that is written as acceptable behavior. Dexter's sister is in love with him, and another character makes a pass at young woman who turned out to be his sperm-donor daughter. Were script consultants hired from Missouri to tap the "Dugger Demographic?"

One of my favorites; Dexter falls hopelessly in love with a female serial killer. In the span of 10 minutes, their affair blossoms to the point he allows her to babysit his toddler son.

Just because I might agree Charles Manson has serious "family values" does not mean I want him babysitting my daughters. I heard John Wayne Gacy did great work as "Pogo the Clown," but would that make him an appropriate choice for a kiddie party? While we're at it, let's have Hannibal Lector cater it.

Unlike Breaking Bad, I think Dexter's writers could have used some of Walter White's product. The writing would have benefitted.

Frank Swanson

Your Teachers Exposed, Volume 1
English Teachers

I've been thinking a lot about teachers these days. There are public perceptions of them that vary wildly from the reality. As an insider, I have taken it upon myself to lift the veil of educational secrecy and reveal the truth in this serial expose. I dedicate the first installment to English teachers.

When someone thinks English teacher, the perceived image is a professional obsessed with dangling participles and finding the true meaning in literature. In reality, they are con artists. They can weave BS into any medium and pass it off as legitimate analysis. They throw in a few fancy words that no one ever uses, like "transcendental" and "post-__________", and presto: their work is done. Watch me do the same thing with a Saturday morning TV show, "Saved By the Bell."

"The character of Screech is a representation of Western Man attempting to find meaning in a post-feminist world. His bungling is symbolic of the male gender trying to redefine himself as a coequal with women. Stripped of his outdated masculinity, Screech's attempts to relate to his peers are awkward when deprived of his patriarchal sphere of comfort."

See, that was easy. I made up a bunch of crap and used the words post, patriarchal, and gender. I can do it again.

"AC Slater is a character that redefines identity politics. Clearly a Latino, he chooses to bury his true ethnicity with an Anglo name. AC Slater stands for those marginalized by mainstream culture; people of color and transgendered populations. The fact that AC Slater is a wrestler underscores his struggle with both his ethnicity and gender preference."

I just called AC Slater a self-loathing homosexual, and by English teacher standards it's totally legit. What about Zach?

"Zach is the embodiment of the Wall Street elite. The fact he can call a 'time out' during the narration, thus breaking story, implies laws do not apply to him. He is always seeking ways to aggrandize himself, often at the expense of his peers. Since he is the only one with a cell phone, that implies the opulent wealth he flagrantly displays before his friends. Zach is clearly a post-transcendental figure that embodies greed, and the politics of the unrestrained ego. The impotent foil for Zach is Principal Belding. Obviously a metaphor for the US government, Belding attempts to reign in Zach's greed and self-serving schemes. Yet, it is Beldon who enables Zach in his quest for self-fulfillment. There are never any real consequences for Zach's behavior, and Beldon is often charmed by his seductive personality. This clearly speaks to the collusion between the US Government and the monied elites who caused the 2008 economic meltdown.

All I would have to do is bake a cake to fully comprehend the literary complexities of Bayside High, and what you have is an English Master's Thesis.

Your Presidential Candidates Vetted, Part I

The fact Donald Trump and Bernie Sanders are at the top of the polls is a testament to my abject failure as an educator. Nobody learned a damned thing, so I have to salvage what is left of my professional dignity by exposing these guys.

The Donald

Donald Trump appeals to late Boomers and Gen Xers who didn't take kindly to book learnin'. Admitting you admire Donald Trump is like coming out of the closet with a mental disability. Those who support his candidacy are determined to "take their country back." From what, I don't know, and I don't think Trump does either.

First, his name is problematic. Anyone with a pronoun for a first name should automatically be disqualified as president. Imagine how it would confuse a generation who already think "YOLO" is a legitimate word. What would we call him?

"Mr. The President, The Donald?"

Second, let's face it. He is a reality star. I'd take a campaign by Uncle Si more seriously. If you thought Putin smacks Obama around like Rhiana, imagine what he would do to Trump?

Putin: "I am going to invade Lithuania."

The Donald: "No you're not because……YOU'RE FIRED!"

Putin chuckles: "Sure, Comrade. I'm fired."

The next day Russian tanks roll through London.

The Donald seems at home ridiculing US POWs, because, "he admired guys who weren't captured." While John McCain languished in a North Vietnamese sweat-box, I suppose the Donald did the same thing at the time—
--except he was in a big, hairy 1970s box belonging to a Champagne hooker named Daphnie.

Bom chika wom-wom.

The Donald is one bad toupee away from being a Monopoly logo. His business decisions prove it. He declared bankruptcy 4 times! And we are supposed to trust him with our national finances? Here are things I'd trust more than Trump with our federal budget:

*Horse-riding lessons with Christopher Reeve.

*Brain surgery performed by Michael J Fox.

*Relationship advice from OJ Simpson.

Bernie Sanders

If there is anything I can say about Bernie, it's that at least he's honest about emulating the economic system of North Korea. In fact, I read his book: <u>Hipster Commie, the Long March Back to Equality</u>. I'll quote the formation of his economic ideas found in Chapter One:

"As a young man, I'll never forget the feast our tribe had after a successful Mammoth hunt. It's where I formed my core beliefs.

I slithered up to our tribal leader, Grog. I told him I felt entitled to a steak too.

With a cold, greedy eye Grog replied: "What did you contribute to the hunt?"

"Well, I scared up a peanut and 2 berries."

"Dufuq 'outta here."

"One-percenter!" I declared. After that, my beloved Lucy starved and died. She now rests in the British Museum. May Global Warming bless her."

Sanders' main support comes from Millennials; the generation weaned on participation trophies. It's no wonder they turned out to be a bunch of Commies! They rot in their parents' basements as they try to market degrees in Trans-Sexual Latin American Authors with a minor in European Porn Studies. Yet, they can't find employment more consequential than "fry salter."

Adventures in Dating: The Instructional Manual

Congratulations on your rental of Cyberdine Systems Model 1970 Frank ®. This instructional manual comes with customer comments and frequently asked questions to give you full use of the Frank.

Frank is a state of the art entertainment system that is regularly updated with factory patches. Intelligent, athletic, and his AI is capable of adapting to meet the needs of our customers.

Customer: "I rented a Frank last weekend for a camping trip. I needed an emotional tampon who would absorb every detail of my ex-husband's crimes both real and imagined. I was unsatisfied."

We are sorry ma'am. What you encountered was a result of advanced AI. Frank doesn't respond to your "damsel-in-distress" bullshit. This is the 21st Century, after all. Please join us. The fact you have no job, no car, and no place 4 years after a divorce is not within Frank's mission parameters.

Customer: "When I introduced him to my gamer son, Sasquatch, Frank didn't seem to want to become an instant baby-daddy for my bastard child. Is there a way he could be reprogrammed for that?"

We are sorry ma'am. We here at Cyberdine have a corporate philosophy that is an integral part of our programming. The ability to wantonly breed for money is frowned upon at our company.

To get full use of your Frank, we recommend frequent maintenance. For a fully functional Frank, he requires the preferred brands of Becks, Heineken, or Ice House for the budget conscious consumer.

Customer: "When we went camping, I let my hair down and drank a lot of beer myself. I think I must have had 3 whole beers! It was crazy! Frank had a lot more. So the next day, I attempted to shame him for it."

Ma'am, do you begrudge how many quarts of oil your car needs for an oil change? Did he drive or do anything that endangered you?

Customer: "Well no, but—"

Then shut the f**k up. We here at Cyberdine Systems cannot be responsible for your Quaker background.

The Frank has detailed files on world and US history. He is happy to share those with anyone who expresses an interest.

Customer: "I don't think that's accurate. I love history too. When I told him about my Ancient Aliens collection, he sort of snuffed and stared at his IPhone."

What you experienced was a firewall, ma'am. It's a defensive mechanism that prevents Stupid Trojan Horses from compromising his internal RAM. Also blocked are: "Ice Road Truckers," "Our Gay Founding Fathers," and Obama speeches.

Customer: "I attempted to stoke the ole romance fires by recalling the many Mongolian orgies I attended at the San Antonio Swingers clubs. After that, he wouldn't touch me."

Franks cannot self-terminate. Included in that are the risks of STD contamination. Cyberdine cannot be held accountable because you chose to live your life as a bipedal sperm bank.

While previous Franks had a military application, the algorithm has embedded itself in the system.

Customer: "When I told him about my friend who shot himself in the leg, he rudely replied, 'That was a negligent discharge. Keep your booger hooks out of the trigger guard until on target.'" That isn't fair. I further tried to explain how my other friend, who knew a lot about guns, had a rifle that went off, he said:

'Are all your friends idiots? Rifles aren't magic.'"

The Cyberdine 1970 model Frank ® is capable of multitasking at a campsite. For optimal performance, the renter is encouraged to help.

Customer: "Well, I didn't have a good time at all. I brought a snack size bag of Cheetos, and I let him set up camp and break it all by himself. In the meantime, I helped myself to all of his food. In fact, the last night we were there, he slept on the innertubes instead of the tent.

Ma'am, according to our records, Frank had entered file-sharing mode. Every unsolicited and illicit photograph you texted was being uploaded to our net, along with a "dependa warning" to other entertainment cyborgs.

We are sorry you didn't enjoy the rental. Considering he paid for EVERYTHING, we here at Cyberdine do not feel you are entitled to a refund.

Here are what other customers thought about renting the Cyberdine 1970 model Frank ®:

"He is a dick"
--Amy.

"I rented a Frank once. But in retrospect, I think he rented me."
--Shirley

"I actually bought a Frank off the factory floor. I traded him in for a one knobbed Etch-a-Sketch. But what do I know? I'm retarded."
--Frank's Ex Wife.

Adventures in Dating: Knocking on Heaven's Door

This happened a couple of months ago, but I'm still laughing about it. I met this girl a while back. We went out a few times, and we had fun. It wasn't a serious relationship, but we generally enjoyed each other's company. Stacey was pretty, single and didn't nurse a drug habit. That set her apart from the usual company I keep; human trash in varying stages of social decay. A couple of months into the courtship—when couples share intimate details—Stacey bet on my basic humanity.

She bet wrong.

Summoning all the courage she could muster, she revealed serious health issues. In addition to Lupus, she had chronic and severe heart disease. The ailments she described sounded like a "House" season finale. And it creeped me out. I don't watch medical oddity shows for a reason. I harbor a deep fear that I'll contract whatever parasite or cancers those shows depict. So imagine my horror with having touched a woman who harbored all of these ways to die. There's no telling what I might catch. After a night with Stacey, I could wake up, and the next thing I know, a f**king alien might burst through my chest. I had no choice. I had to end the courtship.

I did consider the merits of continuing the courtship. There were positives aspects to it. First, I could string her along until the Warcraft expansion comes out this summer. By then, I'm sure she'd be in the last phases of shaking loose her mortal coil. Second, Stacey was like a gallon of milk which means as her expiration dates approaches, I could start cultivating other relationships that didn't involve a threesome with the Grim Reaper. While I enjoy the macabre, I couldn't bring myself to do Death.

Stacey wasn't happy with my choice to end the relationship. She sent a rather obnoxious text registering her displeasure:

"Oh well, it's your loss."

Female logic: She is bedding down for the long nap, and it's MY LOSS? What did she expect; long romantic evenings at the Rheumatologist's office? You know those crappy candy hearts people eat on Valentine's Day? Even those are healthier than hers. Besides, why would I invest in this relationship? It's throwing money away. Spending money on dates with Stacey would be akin to calling a stock broker and putting money down on defunct companies.

"Yeah, I'd like 100 shares on Polaroid. While you're at it, I hear the East India Tea Company is hot."

No I didn't "lose" anything; other than the cost of lilies. I'll take my chances with females who aren't destined to appear on the cover of a Slayer album.

Your Presidential Candidates Vetted, Part II: Chris Christie and Rick Perry

Like most real Americans, I don't want to see the election of Hi lary Clin on (I don't know why, but Word keeps deleting letters when I write her name). But the Republicans remind me of circus clowns spilling out of a tiny car, one more ridiculous than the previous. Here are two of the most obnoxious: Chris Christie and Rick Perry.

Chris Christie

If there is one thing I hate more than a Yankee gun-grabber, it's a Yankee gun-grabber. Christie brings all the style and class we've come to expect from a Craigslist Personal add.

"Man Seeking Nomination:

Big, Beautiful Man seeking to become president. I'm outspoken and direct."

Outspoken and direct translates to crass and fat. That's his personality in a nutshell. He's like that giant woman that starred in the movie Identity Thief; just without the humor. The fact he's built like Dr. Frankenstein stuck a couple of bolts in a Phylli Cheese Steak sandwich and shocked it to life doesn't bother me. It's his obnoxious personality that pisses me off. His presence on the national stage has literally made me racist against fat people. I need to watch that because #fatlivesmatter. I shouldn't worry too much about a President Christie. The only thing trending lower than his poll numbers are his insulin levels.

This gravy-blooded royalty lords over New Jersey, and it should repulse most Americans. It's historical fact; nothing good has come from New Jersey. Ever. His constituents are spray-tanned Rachel Dolezal clones with nasally accents. No doubt he'll staff his administration with these types. It'll be like a 4th season of Jersey Shore. The Situation returns as Secretary of State. His trademark will be flashing his abs and drooling when an international crisis emerges. Treasury Secretary J-WoW breaks our economy on a shoe-buying spree.

For the love all that is right in America, we have to stop this MTV wreck before it starts.

Rick Perry

Rick Perry is so humorless and dour he could be an Adam Sandler movie. Texas teachers hate this guy. He is the dentist to our lion. The only thing he accomplished for Texas education was the construction of football stadiums to please our pig-skinned gods. To fully explain my hatred in lay-person terms,

I'll have to do it via Star Wars.

Episode IV : A "NO" Hope:

Obi-Wan: "For a thousand generations, Texas teachers were the guardians of knowledge and civilization in our republic. That was before the dark times; before the Perry."

Teach Skywalker: "How did my paycheck die?"

Obi-Wan: "A pupil of mine named Rick Perry. He was seduced by the Cretin."

Teach Skywalker: "The Cretin?"

Obi-Wan: "The Cretin is a blanket of stupidity that re-elects Perry and now accounts for the Donald's surge in the polls."

Scene shifts to a Football Stadium converted to a planet-destroying space station. Aboard are Rick Perry and Princess Leia.
Leia: "Please don't blow up the public school system. We are doing our best with what…"
Rick Perry: "Do you have another target? A charter-school target?"
Leia: "No, but charter teachers work for slave wages. If you give us—"
BOOM!

After Rick Perry's departure as governor, we can now look forward to the hijinks of "Jar-Jar Abbot." Thus far, his claim to Texas' safety and security is in his proclamation: "Meesa thinks-a the US Army is going to enslave Texas!"

Frank Swanson

Barracks Tales, Part 2: Welcome to the Battalion

My first experience at my gaining command consisted of me and three other guys sitting in a conference room. We were new to the unit, and the Battalion CO wanted to impart his words of wisdom. By words of wisdom, I imagine he wanted to reinforce the one golden rule of any military unit; don't be an idiot. I know--it sounds like common sense--but the average civilian would be surprised how we win wars with so many retards in our ranks.

The CO arrived. After the obligatory "Attention on Deck," he began his canned speech to us potential morons. Drinking and Driving is bad. Assault and rape are bad. Sexual harassment and racism are bad. Despite his boredom during the affair, he seemed keen on one potential subject; the dangers of Tijuana. You have to understand something; outside of every military base in the Free World, there is always that one PLACE. That one PLACE is usually restricted, but still harvests hundreds of GIs every weekend. That one PLACE is a whore house. Outside of Fort Leonard Wood, it was "Daisey's Health Spa." Staffed by an 80 year old, toothless Chinese woman, "Daisey's Heath Spa" hosted the most wretched prostitutes in all of world history.

Tijuana was that PLACE for the Navy and the Marine Corps stationed in San Diego. A border town that served as the inspiration for Mos Eisley, Tijuana indulged every sin imaginable in an otherwise Catholic country. After a lengthy horror story comparing a Mexican border town to Camp Crystal Lake, the CO brought in a Navy SEAL to punctuate the dangers that awaited us.

"Yes," the SEAL addressed us. "Tijuana is hazardous. As the CO already pointed out, we can't forbid you to go, but it is dangerous. I was led into an alley and severely beat by a gang of Mexicans. It was so bad, I spent the next six weeks in the hospital."

Wait a minute, I think. Navy SEALS are like the James Bonds of popular imagination. And yet this dick was lured into a dark alley on the ruse of cheap beer or child sex?

Worst.

SEAL

Ever.

When the presentation concluded, the CO and his pet SEAL left us in the conference room. It was near 17:00, the end of the work day—on a Friday. One of the guys, Kurt, turns to me and asks, "So what are we going to do this weekend?"

We scratch our heads, while weighing our personal safety versus our need to explore Donkey shows and hookers. Satisfied that sounded more amusing than Disneyland or Sea World, we agree:

"Fuck it! Let's go to Tijuana!"

We agreed to rendezvous for our journey by 8:00 that evening. Kurt picked me up and we head over to Dave's barracks. Dave is an interesting train-wreck of a human, whose self-loathing peeks during off duty hours. First, he looked like Beavis. No shit, to think

Mike Judge plagiarized God, and cursed this man to look like a cartoon was enough to make anyone doubt Divine Mercy. Second, as a prior-service Marine, Dave had married a Filipino woman whose value could be measured as a prize in a shady game of back alley craps. It was a symbiotic relationship; she got a ticket out of Third World poverty, and he got to assume a flimsy veil of normality. By the time we arrived, Dave had consumed an entire 12 pack of beer in 2 hours. Yes, to kick off a night of drinking, Dave warmed up to a blood alcohol level of .35. He had already began speaking in tongues:

"When ve geet tooo Tijuwana, I'm gonna fist fuck all 'dem bitches."

The night started off at Taco Bell. No, it wasn't a corporate-licensed Taco Bell, just a Third World shithole of a restaurant whose sole purpose was to hoodwink the drunks into thinking they were eating something approved by the FDA. Despite the dirt floor, and the shit smeared on the walls, it was good.

"I wonder what kind of meat are in these tacos?" I asked.

"There's your answer." Kurt replied, pointing out of the window where a three-legged dog scampered across the street.

As we wove our way through the twisted maze of crowded streets, punctuated with beggars, child prostitutes, and gold vendors, we arrived at our destination—Revolution Street. The name alone holds a weight of notoriety for anyone who's been there. It makes Las Vegas look like a daycare center.

We venture into our first strip club. As a seasoned veteran of Tijuana, Kurt offers some advice: "Anything goes here. Be careful not to hook up with a tranny."

"I'm gonna fuck blurp," *hiccup* "some bitches." Dave slurred. At this point, I doubt he'll live.

I take my seat, and I'm immediately swarmed with women who are so weathered and beaten, that I'm sure their day job consisted of harvesting vegetables in Baja California. I wave most of them away when I declare, "Soy casado. Estoy en amor con mi esposa. Quiero tomar cervesa, solamente."

I'm married, and love my wife. I'm only here to drink beer.

That didn't sway one, determined whore. Deftly she reached into my pants, her big, meaty claws awkwardly trying to stroke my shaft. Her sand-papery palms, borne of long hours picking tomatoes, scratch and burn. Normally, I'm not a nice person. Add a couple of beers and surround me with people that fail to make the cut of homo sapiens, I become a real asshole. I jerked her hand out of my pants and used it as a club to strike her in the face three or four times. She yelped and scurried away.

Dave disappeared. Fifteen minutes later, he emerged from the back of the club; that's where the cubbies are where the customers fuck the stripper/hookers. With a smile on his cartoon face, he waved a napkin as proudly as Neil Armstrong did our flag.

"I fucked her. Beat that, mother fuckers….and she gave me her number. We're going to go out next weekend."

I look at the napkin. "Dave, there are three numbers on it."

"It's her phone number, and we are going out."

"Ok Bill, whatever you say." Kurt added. "Let's go to a better bar."

Our next stop was a slightly better whorehouse. I sat, content to drink beer and watch semi-clothed hookers dance for our amusement. I had no intention of cheating on my wife, especially with toothless Turd Worlders. Then, I saw her.

On the main stage, strutted one of the most beautiful women I had ever seen in my life; toned legs, a perfect olive complexion, smoky brown eyes and full lips framed by jet black hair that flowed gracefully as she danced. Time froze. I could not take my eyes off her. The whole fucking world could have caught fire, and I wouldn't have cared in the slightest.

She looked EXACTLY like Elvira, Mistress of the Dark.

You have to understand something. I have a decades-long crush on Elvira. She was a horror show host in the early 80s, right about the time I discovered my dick did more than pee. I'd tune in every Saturday night to watch her. Afterward, I'd take all that pent up horniness and express it all over my pillow. I spilled so much seed over her that I could have repopulated the continent of Australia—twice over.   And here she was, just feet away.

Please don't come over here. But do come over here. I'm married.

Fate decided for me. Not only did she come over to my table, she perched herself on my lap. She smelled sweet, a mix of strawberry shampoo and a hint of perfume. Her green eyes locked onto mine. I was harder than Chinese math. I felt lightheaded as every drop of blood in my body rushed into my dick. If my erection were any harder, I'm sure I could have turned myself inside out.

She knew it too. "You like me?"

In that instant I went from bilingual, Cum Laude College Graduate to window-licking idiot. I stuttered something that might have been a yes. I'm not sure. She leaned in and kissed me. Have you ever had a moment so perfect that your whole life can be judged by it? Here I was, a thousand miles away from home, in a Mexican whorehouse with a sexual fantasy perched on my lap. I look over to my friends. Dave was prattling to a whore about his girlfriend from the other bar. Kurt and a hooker sat next to me; a tangle of arms and legs in such a puzzle, that I couldn't tell where she began and he ended.

Elvira kissed me again. "I like you. $40 and you can do whatever you want to me."

I suppose Kurt heard her offer, and judging by the wistful look on my face, he fished out two twenty dollar bills and handed them to me. That's the main thing I miss about the military; your friends are your brothers, and they always take care of you.

She took me hand and led me away, to the fuck cubbies. I could barely walk, crippled by a raging hard on that could have cut diamonds. Then it happened;

Flashes of my little girls pop into my head. I couldn't do it. They depended on a father to be responsible, and committed to a stable home. And as much as every part of me wanted to crawl up inside her vagina and nest, I just couldn't do it.

"Yo no puedo." I sighed.

I can't do this.

Elvira asked why.

"I'm married. I love my family, and I can't."

She smiled and gave me one last peck on the cheek. "Your wife is a lucky woman. I hope she appreciates you." She hugged me and walked away.

I hate morals.

Needless to say, once the night was over and I was alone in my room I spent the entire next day masturbating so furiously that I painted the walls in seaman and blood. It looked like a crime scene.

The story has a post script. I atoned for my morality after my divorce with a trip to Jamaica. There, I reached such depraved depths that I had to redefine shame, even by my own generous standards. Oh yeah, and I needed a blood test.

But that is another story…

Police Academy: An 80s Movie with a Copaganda Problem

I've gone a renaissance of 80s movies that, as a child, I found entertaining. Fast forward a few decades, wars, recessions, and pandemics later, and I discovered something.

They weren't funny. Not in the slightest.

I rewatched Police Academy on Netflix, because that is about the quality I expect from them. I found a lot of this movie tone deaf to modern sensibilities, and why it's playing on Netflix is beyond me. Allow me to point out how this movie fails the test of time.

The most egregious scene was one where a cadet was studying. How illiterate do you have to be to study in a police academy? They only have 3 functions: beat people, shoot people, and run away. What volumes of Aristotle-like wisdom do you need for that?

The racism is thick in this movie. It's as if the writers were afraid if they didn't pen a racial slur every ten minutes the target Boomer audience would lose interest. Racial epithets are paired with racial stereotypes to keep the laughs rolling when this piece of shit debuted in Klan bars. The character of Hightower, played by Bubba Smith, is a combination of "strong black guy" tropes with a reassuring "he's one of the good ones" for the Boomers who enjoyed this shit. For the ladies who once swooned over Paul McCartney, there is the character of George Martin, a white guy playing a Latino whose joke is: "Look at me. I'm Latin and I fuck a lot of girls."

Funny?

Please, laugh.

The character of Tackelberry is the worst offender and a shining example for American police. He exemplifies the duality found within cops right before they kill your dog or assassinate a homeless guy for loitering. The joke here is Tackleberry likes guns. I mean he really likes guns. In one scene he is going through a mock town and he shoots up civilians and criminals alike. He does not discern one from the other. As a reward, he is celebrated for his "us" vs "them" take when interacting with civilians. I think we can all agree this is how police operate unless there is an active shooter. Then the thin blue line turns yellow as children die.

Yeah, I hate this movie.